# American Idioms Handbook

Build Your Vocabulary with Powerful Sayings, Expressions, and Phrases through Examples, and Learn About Their Origins

Polly Proverberson

# Contents

# Chapter 1

# Welcome to the World of Idioms

## What Are Idioms?

Idioms are fascinating linguistic expressions that color our everyday language, adding vibrancy and cultural depth to communication. They are phrases or expressions whose meanings cannot be deduced from the literal definitions of the individual words that make them up. Instead, idioms have developed meanings that are understood through common usage within a particular language or culture.

Imagine hearing someone say, "It's raining cats and dogs." If taken literally, this phrase would conjure up a bizarre image of animals falling from the sky. However, as an idiom, it simply means that it is raining very heavily. Similarly, if someone tells you to "break a leg" before a performance, they are not wishing you harm but rather conveying good luck.

Idioms are integral to the richness and fluidity of a language. They often reflect historical events, cultural norms, and societal values. For example, the idiom "barking up the wrong tree" has its origins in hunting dogs that would mistakenly bark at the base of the wrong tree, thinking their prey was there. Over time, it has come to mean pursuing a mistaken or misguided course of action.

Idioms can be categorized in various ways:

- **Pure idioms:** These are phrases with meanings that are completely different from the literal interpretation of the words. For example, "kick the bucket" means to die, not to literally kick a bucket.

- **Semi-idioms:** These expressions have at least one word that retains its literal meaning. For example, "make ends meet" means to have enough money to cover your expenses. "Ends" and "meet" retain some literal sense.

- **Literal idioms:** These are phrases that are understood by their literal meaning and are commonly used. For instance, "spill the beans" means to reveal a secret, where the act of spilling can be taken both literally and figuratively.

Idioms often make language learning more challenging because their meanings are not immediately obvious. Yet, they are an essential part of mastering a language, providing insight into the culture and everyday lives of its speakers.

## Why Learn Idioms?

Learning idioms is crucial for anyone striving to achieve fluency in a new language, particularly English. Here are several reasons why idioms are important:

**Enhancing Communication Skills** Idioms are ubiquitous in everyday conversation, media, literature, and even in professional settings. A good grasp of idioms allows for more natural and engaging communication. They enable speakers to express complex ideas succinctly and colorfully. For example, saying "the ball is in your court" conveys the idea that it is someone else's turn to take action, in a way that is more vivid and relatable than a straightforward statement.

**Cultural Understanding** Idioms often reflect the cultural heritage and values of a society. By learning idioms, one gains insight into the history, humor, and traditions of English-speaking cultures. For instance, the idiom "a stitch in time saves nine" reflects a practical, industrious mindset, emphasizing the importance of timely action to prevent bigger problems.

**Improving Listening Comprehension** Native speakers frequently use idioms, especially in informal settings. Understanding idiomatic expressions is essential for comprehending movies, TV shows, songs, and conversations. Without this knowledge, even advanced learners can find themselves puzzled by otherwise familiar words arranged in unfamiliar ways.

**Enhancing Writing Skills** Using idioms appropriately can make writing more compelling and relatable. Whether crafting a story, an essay, or a business report, idioms can add a layer of expressiveness. However, it's important to use them judiciously and appropriately to avoid confusion or seeming overly informal in more formal writing contexts.

**Fostering Social Connections** Shared idioms can serve as a bonding tool, fostering a sense of camaraderie among speakers. They can break the ice in conversations, provide common ground, and convey emotions or thoughts more effectively. When a non-native speaker uses idioms correctly, it can also signal a higher level of language proficiency, earning respect and admiration from native speakers.

**Boosting Confidence** Mastery of idioms can significantly boost a language learner's confidence. Knowing that you can understand and use idiomatic expressions correctly can reduce anxiety in social interactions and help you feel more at ease when speaking or listening to native speakers.

## The Importance of Idioms in Different Contexts

Idioms permeate various aspects of life, and their importance varies across different contexts. Here are a few key areas where idioms play a significant role:

**Everyday Conversations** In daily interactions, idioms help convey thoughts and feelings more vividly. Expressions like "hit the hay" for going to bed, or "burning the midnight oil" for staying up late working, add color and personality to conversations.

**Media and Literature** Idioms are a staple in media and literature. They enrich dialogues in movies, TV shows, and books, making characters more relatable and their speech more natural. For instance, in the Harry Potter series, J.K. Rowling uses idioms like "when pigs fly" to signify something impossible, enhancing the magical yet familiar world she creates.

**Business and Professional Settings** In the workplace, idioms can be useful for succinctly expressing ideas and fostering teamwork. Phrases like "think outside the box" or "hit the ground running" are common in business jargon, encouraging creativity and proactive behavior.

**Academic Writing** While idioms are generally more common in spoken language and informal writing, they can also be used in academic writing to some extent. When used appropriately, they can illustrate points more effectively. For example, "a double-edged sword" can describe a situation with both positive and negative outcomes.

## Strategies for Learning Idioms

Learning idioms can be challenging, but with the right strategies, it can also be enjoyable and rewarding. Here are some tips to help you master idiomatic expressions:

**1. Contextual Learning** Understanding the context in which an idiom is used is crucial. Idioms are often tied to specific situations or cultural references, so seeing them in action helps solidify their meanings and proper usage.

- **Watch Movies and TV Shows:** Pay attention to how characters use idioms in dialogues. Note the situations and emotions associated with the idioms.
- **Read Books and Articles:** Literature and articles are rich sources of idiomatic expressions. Highlight idioms you encounter and jot down their meanings.
- **Listen to Native Speakers:** Engage in conversations with native speakers or listen to podcasts and radio shows. Hearing idioms used naturally reinforces your understanding.

**2. Practice Regularly** Repetition is key to mastering any aspect of language. Regular practice helps move idioms from short-term to long-term memory.

- **Daily Idiom Challenge:** Learn a new idiom each day and use it in a sentence or conversation.
- **Review Sessions:** Regularly review idioms you've learned to keep them fresh in your mind. Use flashcards or a dedicated notebook for this purpose.
- **Language Exchange:** Partner with a language exchange buddy and challenge each other to use idioms in your conversations.

**3. Use Mnemonics and Visuals** Mnemonics are memory aids that help you recall information more easily. Creating vivid mental images can make idioms more memorable.

- **Create Visual Associations:** Draw pictures or find images online that represent the idioms. For example, visualize someone literally "barking up the wrong tree" to remember its meaning.
- **Storytelling:** Create short stories or scenarios that incorporate idioms. The narrative context can help you remember the idioms better.

**4. Group Idioms by Theme** Categorizing idioms by theme or topic can make them easier to learn and remember. Grouping idioms with similar meanings or contexts helps reinforce their usage.

- **Thematic Lists:** Create lists of idioms based on common themes, such as time, money, emotions, etc.
- **Mind Maps:** Use mind maps to connect related idioms visually. This method helps you see relationships between different expressions.

**5. Use them regularly!:** Active use of idioms in speaking and writing reinforces your learning. The more you use idioms, the more natural they will become.

- **Write Essays or Stories:** Add these idioms into your writing assignments. This practice helps you think creatively about how to use them appropriately.
- **Practice Dialogues:** Write dialogues that include idioms. Practicing these conversations helps you become more comfortable using idioms in speech.
- **Public Speaking:** If you have opportunities for public speaking, challenge yourself to include idioms in your speeches. This practice builds confidence and fluency.

**6. Interactive Learning Tools** Leverage interactive tools and resources to make learning idioms more engaging.

- **Flashcards:** Create physical or digital flashcards with idioms on one side and meanings on the other. Quiz yourself regularly.
- **Language Apps:** Use language learning apps that focus on idioms and expressions. There are a lot of apps available that can make learning fun.
- **Online Forums:** Join online forums or social media groups focused on language learning. Participate in discussions and share idioms with other learners.

**7. Focus on High-Frequency Idioms** Start with idioms that are commonly used in everyday language. These high-frequency idioms will be most useful in daily conversations and are often easier to remember.

- **Top 100 Lists:** Many language resources provide lists of the most commonly used idioms. Focus on these lists as a starting point.
- **Frequency Dictionaries:** Consider using frequency dictionaries that highlight idiomatic expressions based on their usage in real-life language.

**8. Use Technology Wisely** Technology offers numerous tools to aid in language learning. Incorporate these tools into your study routine.

- **Language Learning Apps:** Apps like Anki, Quizlet, and Memrise allow you to create and study flashcards on the go.
- **Speech Recognition Software:** Use software that helps you practice pronunciation and usage of idioms in context.
- **Digital Notebooks:** Keep a digital notebook or journal to track the idioms you learn and your progress over time.

**9. Understand the Cultural Context** Idioms are deeply rooted in the culture of a language. Understanding the cultural context can enhance your comprehension and appreciation of idiomatic expressions.

- **Cultural Immersion:** Immerse yourself in the culture where the language is spoken. Watch local TV shows, follow news channels, and read books that reflect the culture.
- **Historical Background:** Learn about the historical events and

societal trends that gave rise to certain idioms. This knowledge can provide deeper insights into their meanings.

**10. Seek Feedback and Guidance** Getting feedback from native speakers or language experts can be invaluable in mastering idioms.

- **Language Tutors:** Consider working with a language tutor who can provide personalized feedback on your use of idioms.
- **Peer Reviews:** Engage in peer review sessions with fellow learners. Discuss and critique each other's use of idioms in writing and speech.
- **Language Workshops:** Attend workshops or classes focused on idiomatic expressions and their usage.

**11. Keep a Learning Journal** Maintaining a learning journal can help you track your progress and reflect on your learning journey.

- **Daily Entries:** Write daily entries that include the idioms you've learned, how you've used them, and any challenges you've faced.
- **Reflection:** Reflect on your learning strategies and adjust them as needed. Note which methods work best for you and which areas need more focus.
- **Goal Setting:** Set specific, achievable goals for learning idioms. Review and adjust these goals regularly to keep your learning on track.

**12. Enjoy the Process** Finally, remember that learning idioms should be an enjoyable and enriching experience. Embrace the quirks and humor of idiomatic expressions and have fun with the learning process.

- **Stay Curious:** Cultivate a sense of curiosity and wonder about language. Enjoy discovering new idioms and their meanings.
- **Celebrate Milestones:** Celebrate your achievements and milestones in your idiom-learning journey. Reward yourself for reaching your goals.
- **Stay Positive:** Keep a positive attitude and don't be discouraged by setbacks. Language learning is a gradual process, and every step forward is progress.

By following these tips and techniques, you'll find that learning idioms becomes a rewarding and enjoyable part of your language journey. Remember, the key to mastering idioms is consistent practice, exposure, and a genuine interest in the language and culture.

## How to Use This Book

This book is designed to be a comprehensive guide, offering you not just the meanings of idioms but also insights into their origins, contexts, and practical applications. To make the most of this book, it's essential to understand its structure and how best to navigate its contents.

### Understanding the Structure

The book is divided into several parts, each focusing on different aspects of idioms. Here's a brief overview:

- **Everyday Idioms:** This section covers idioms you might encounter in daily conversations. These are essential for understanding casual speech and engaging in small talk.
- **Descriptive Idioms:** This part focuses on idioms used to describe people, places, and things. It's particularly useful for adding color to your descriptions and making your language more vivid.
- **Action Idioms:** Here, you'll find idioms related to actions and behaviors, commonly used in various scenarios, including work and study.
- **Fun and Playful Idioms:** This section includes idioms related to sports, games, food, and celebrations, perfect for adding a playful tone to your conversations.
- **Specialized Idioms:** This part explores idioms from pop culture and history, providing context for how these expressions have evolved and their significance.
- **Regional Idioms:** Here, you'll discover idioms specific to different regions of the United States, offering a glimpse into regional linguistic quirks.
- **Practice and Application:** This section is designed to help you practice using idioms in writing and speech, with exercises, prompts, and tips for effective communication.
- **Resources:** At the end of the book, you'll find a comprehensive reference list, indexes, and additional resources for further learning.

**Navigating the Book**

To help you find what you need quickly, each chapter begins with an introduction outlining the key idioms and their contexts. The idioms are organized alphabetically within each chapter, making it easy to look up specific expressions. Additionally, the book includes cross-references to related idioms and themes, so you can explore connections between different expressions.

Use the indexes at the end of the book to search for idioms by keyword or theme. This is particularly useful if you remember part of an idiom but need to find the full expression and its meaning.

**Engaging with Examples**

Each idiom is accompanied by multiple examples to show you how it's used in context. These examples are drawn from everyday conversation, literature, media, and professional settings. Pay attention to these examples, as they will help you understand the nuances of each idiom and how to use it appropriately.

**Practice Sections**

At the end of each chapter, you'll find practice sections designed to reinforce your learning. These include:

- **Fill-in-the-Blank Exercises:** These exercises help you test your understanding by filling in missing idioms in sentences.
- **Matching Exercises:** Match idioms to their meanings to reinforce your memory.
- **Writing Prompts:** Use idioms in your own sentences and short

paragraphs to practice incorporating them into your writing.

- **Conversation Starters:** Practice using idioms in dialogue with these conversation starters.

### Cultural Insights

Understanding the cultural context behind idioms can deepen your appreciation and mastery of them. Throughout the book, you'll find cultural notes that explain the historical and societal background of various idioms. These insights not only make learning more interesting but also help you understand why certain expressions are used.

### Glossary and Appendices

The glossary provides definitions and examples of all the idioms covered in the book. Use it as a quick reference tool when you encounter an unfamiliar idiom. The appendices include categorized lists of idioms (e.g., by theme, frequency of use), which can be helpful for focused study.

By following these guidelines and making use of the book's features, you'll be well-equipped to navigate the world of idioms confidently and effectively.

Chapter 2

# Common Phrases for Daily Conversation

Idioms are a significant part of any language, adding flavor, depth, and cultural nuances to conversations. Mastering common idiomatic expressions can enhance your ability to communicate effectively and naturally. This chapter focuses on idioms used in daily conversations, specifically in greetings, goodbyes, small talk, and expressing emotions. We will also include interactive exercises and Fun Facts to make learning engaging and memorable.

## Greetings and Goodbyes

Greetings and farewells are essential components of social interactions. They set the tone for the conversation and help establish rapport. Using idiomatic expressions in greetings and goodbyes can make these exchanges warmer and more engaging.

## 1. Greetings

### Break the Ice

- **Meaning:** To initiate conversation in a social setting, making people feel more comfortable.
- **Example:** "She told a funny story to break the ice at the beginning of the meeting."
- **Usage:** Often used when meeting new people or starting a conversation in a group setting. It suggests using a friendly gesture or comment to ease any initial awkwardness.

### What's Up?

- **Meaning:** A casual way to ask someone how they are or what they are doing.
- **Example:** "Hey, what's up? Haven't seen you in a while."
- **Usage:** Informal greeting commonly used among friends and acquaintances. Versatile and suitable for various casual settings.

### Long Time No See

- **Meaning:** A friendly way to greet someone you haven't seen in a while.
- **Example:** "Long time no see! How have you been?"
- **Usage:** Used when running into someone after a significant period of not seeing them. Conveys happy surprise and interest in catching

up.

**How's It Going?**

- **Meaning:** Another way to ask someone how they are doing.
- **Example:** "How's it going? Everything okay?"
- **Usage:** Casual greeting suitable for everyday use with friends, family, or colleagues.

**Good to See You**

- **Meaning:** A polite and warm way to acknowledge someone's presence.
- **Example:** "Good to see you, John! How have you been?"
- **Usage:** Conveys warmth and friendliness, often used in slightly more formal or professional settings.

**Look Who It Is!**

- **Meaning:** An enthusiastic way to greet someone, showing surprise and pleasure.
- **Example:** "Look who it is! I haven't seen you in ages."
- **Usage:** Used when unexpectedly meeting someone you know and like, adding a touch of excitement to the greeting.

**Make Someone's Day**

- **Meaning:** To make someone very happy.

- **Example:** "Your surprise visit really made my day!"
- **Usage:** Used to describe the effect of a positive action or event on someone's mood.

**Hello Stranger**

- **Meaning:** A friendly greeting for someone you haven't seen in a while.
- **Example:** "Hello stranger! Where have you been hiding?"
- **Usage:** Informal and playful, often used among friends.

**What's New?**

- **Meaning:** Asking for the latest news or updates from someone.
- **Example:** "Hey, what's new with you?"
- **Usage:** Casual way to prompt someone to share recent happenings.

**How Have You Been?**

- **Meaning:** Asking about someone's well-being over a period of time.
- **Example:** "How have you been since we last met?"
- **Usage:** Slightly more formal, used when you haven't seen someone in a while.

## 2. Goodbyes

### Catch You Later

- **Meaning:** A casual way to say goodbye, implying you will see the person again soon.
- **Example:** "I've got to run. Catch you later!"
- **Usage:** Informal farewell often used among friends and peers. Conveys a sense of ongoing connection.

### Take Care

- **Meaning:** A caring way to say goodbye, wishing the person well.
- **Example:** "It was nice seeing you. Take care!"
- **Usage:** Suitable for both casual and semi-formal farewells. Shows concern for the person's well-being.

### Have a Good One

- **Meaning:** A casual way to wish someone well as they leave.
- **Example:** "I'm heading out now. Have a good one!"
- **Usage:** Versatile idiom used in various contexts, typically in casual settings.

### See You Around

- **Meaning:** A casual way to say goodbye, implying you will see the person again in the future.

- **Example:** "I have to go now. See you around!"
- **Usage:** Often used in casual conversations with acquaintances or colleagues.

**I'm Off**

- **Meaning:** A casual way to announce you are leaving.
- **Example:** "It's getting late. I'm off. See you tomorrow."
- **Usage:** Commonly used when leaving a place or event. Straightforward and to the point.

**Until Next Time**

- **Meaning:** A polite way to say goodbye, implying you will see the person again.
- **Example:** "Thanks for everything. Until next time!"
- **Usage:** Often used in semi-formal or formal contexts. Indicates a positive expectation of future meetings.

**Take It Easy**

- **Meaning:** A relaxed way to say goodbye, suggesting the person should relax and not stress.
- **Example:** "I'm heading home. Take it easy!"
- **Usage:** Typically used among friends or in informal settings. Conveys a laid-back attitude.

**Farewell**

- **Meaning:** A formal way to say goodbye.
- **Example:** "Farewell, my friend. Safe travels."
- **Usage:** Often used in more formal or emotional contexts. Carries a sense of finality and good wishes.

**See You Later, Alligator**

- **Meaning:** A playful and rhyming way to say goodbye.
- **Example:** "See you later, alligator!"
- **Usage:** Often used with children or in a fun, light-hearted context.

**Peace Out**

- **Meaning:** A very casual way to say goodbye.
- **Example:** "I'm off. Peace out!"
- **Usage:** Commonly used among younger people or in very informal settings.

**Adios**

- **Meaning:** A Spanish word for goodbye, commonly used in English as a casual farewell.
- **Example:** "Adios! See you tomorrow."
- **Usage:** Informal, often used with a bit of flair or humor.

**Practical Tips for Using Greeting and Goodbye Idioms:**

- **Match the Tone:** Choose your idioms based on the formality of the situation and your relationship with the person. Casual greetings are best for friends and peers, while more formal ones are suitable for professional settings.
- **Be Contextual:** Pay attention to the context of the conversation. For instance, "Long time no see" is only appropriate if you actually haven't seen the person in a while.
- **Practice:** Try using different idioms in various situations to become comfortable with them. The more you practice, the more natural they will feel.

## Small Talk

Small talk is an essential social skill that helps build connections and ease into more substantial conversations. Idioms can make small talk more engaging and expressive. This section covers common idioms used in small talk, from discussing the weather to talking about plans and interests.

## 1. Talking About the Weather

### Under the Weather

- **Meaning:** Feeling ill.
- **Example:** "I'm feeling a bit under the weather today."
- **Usage:** Used to explain why you might not be at your best. Subtle way to indicate you're not feeling well without going into detail.

### It's Raining Cats and Dogs

- **Meaning:** It's raining very heavily.
- **Example:** "I can't believe how hard it's raining outside. It's raining cats and dogs!"
- **Usage:** Commonly used to describe intense rainstorms. Vivid way to talk about the weather.

### A Cold Snap

- **Meaning:** A sudden brief period of cold weather.
- **Example:** "We're expecting a cold snap this weekend, so bundle up."

- **Usage:** Useful for discussing sudden changes in weather, particularly in colder climates.

**In the Dog Days**

- **Meaning:** The hottest days of summer.
- **Example:** "We're in the dog days of summer, and it's sweltering outside."
- **Usage:** Typically used to describe the peak of summer heat. Often associated with a sense of lethargy due to the extreme temperatures.

**Come Rain or Shine**

- **Meaning:** No matter the circumstances, regardless of the weather.
- **Example:** "We'll go hiking this weekend, come rain or shine."
- **Usage:** Expresses determination to do something regardless of external conditions.

**A Scorcher**

- **Meaning:** An extremely hot day.
- **Example:** "It's a real scorcher out there today!"
- **Usage:** Describing very hot weather.

## 2. Discussing Interests and Hobbies

### Hit the Books

- **Meaning:** To study very hard.
- **Example:** "I've got exams next week, so it's time to hit the books."
- **Usage:** Commonly used among students or when discussing academic efforts.

### Couch Potato

- **Meaning:** A person who spends a lot of time sitting and watching television.
- **Example:** "I've been a real couch potato lately, just binge-watching shows."
- **Usage:** Often used humorously to describe someone's lazy habits.

### Read Between the Lines

- **Meaning:** To understand the hidden meaning or implication.
- **Example:** "If you read between the lines, you'll see that she's not really happy with her job."
- **Usage:** Useful for discussing deeper meanings or underlying messages in conversations.

### Bite Off More Than You Can Chew

- **Meaning:** To take on more responsibility than one can handle.

- **Example:** "I think I bit off more than I can chew by signing up for three extra classes."
- **Usage:** Often used to discuss the challenges of overcommitment.

**Burn the Midnight Oil**

- **Meaning:** To work late into the night.
- **Example:** "I had to burn the midnight oil to finish the project on time."
- **Usage:** Common in discussions about work or study habits, particularly when talking about long hours.

**Jam Session**

- **Meaning:** An informal gathering of musicians to play music together.
- **Example:** "We're having a jam session at my place tonight. Want to join?"
- **Usage:** Used in musical contexts, often casually.

**Bookworm**

- **Meaning:** A person who loves to read.
- **Example:** "She's such a bookworm; she spends all her free time reading."
- **Usage:** Often used to describe someone's reading habits.

## 3. Sharing Plans and Future Events

### In the Pipeline

- **Meaning:** In progress or about to happen.
- **Example:** "We have several new projects in the pipeline for next year."
- **Usage:** Often used in professional contexts to discuss upcoming plans or developments.

### Down the Road

- **Meaning:** In the future.
- **Example:** "We might consider expanding our business down the road."
- **Usage:** Useful for discussing long-term plans or future possibilities.

### Call It a Day

- **Meaning:** To stop working for the day.
- **Example:** "We've done enough work today; let's call it a day."
- **Usage:** Often used at the end of a workday or after completing a significant task.

### Up in the Air

- **Meaning:** Uncertain or undecided.

- **Example:** "Our travel plans are still up in the air due to the pandemic."
- **Usage:** Used to describe situations that are not yet finalized or are subject to change.

### Pulling Strings

- **Meaning:** Using influence to get something done.
- **Example:** "She got the promotion by pulling some strings with the management."
- **Usage:** Commonly used in discussions about achieving goals through connections or influence.

### In the Works

- **Meaning:** In the process of being planned or developed.
- **Example:** "We have a new product in the works."
- **Usage:** Often used in business or project planning contexts.

### On the Horizon

- **Meaning:** Likely to happen or appear soon.
- **Example:** "There's a big promotion on the horizon."
- **Usage:** Used to describe upcoming events or changes.

## 4. Engaging in Light Conversation

### Chew the Fat

- **Meaning:** To have a casual conversation.
- **Example:** "We spent the afternoon chewing the fat about our college days."
- **Usage:** Perfect for describing relaxed, informal conversations.

### Shoot the Breeze

- **Meaning:** To chat informally.
- **Example:** "They were just shooting the breeze, talking about their weekend plans."
- **Usage:** Often used to describe casual, unstructured conversations.

### Beat Around the Bush

- **Meaning:** To avoid getting to the point.
- **Example:** "Stop beating around the bush and tell me what happened."
- **Usage:** Used when someone is not addressing the main issue directly.

### Get the Ball Rolling

- **Meaning:** To start something, especially a project or process.

- **Example:** "Let's get the ball rolling on this new initiative."
- **Usage:** Commonly used in professional settings to indicate the beginning of a task or project.

**Touch Base**

- **Meaning:** To briefly make contact with someone.
- **Example:** "I'll touch base with you next week to see how the project is going."
- **Usage:** Often used in business contexts to suggest checking in with someone.

**Catch Up**

- **Meaning:** To talk with someone you haven't seen for a while and learn what they have been doing.
- **Example:** "Let's meet for coffee and catch up."
- **Usage:** Commonly used among friends or acquaintances.

**Practical Tips for Using Small Talk Idioms:**

- **Be Natural:** Use idioms that feel natural to you and fit your speaking style. Forced usage can come across as awkward.
- **Know Your Audience:** Tailor your idiom usage to the familiarity and comfort level of your audience. Some idioms may be too casual for certain settings.
- **Mix and Match:** Combine idioms with regular speech to keep the

conversation flowing smoothly. Overusing idioms can make your speech sound contrived.

- **Practice in Real Conversations:** The best way to become comfortable with idioms is to use them in real-life conversations. Pay attention to how native speakers use them and try to mimic their usage.

## Expressing Emotions

Expressing emotions accurately and vividly is crucial in any language. Idioms can add depth and color to your emotional expressions, making your communication more impactful and relatable. Here are some common idioms for expressing emotions:

### 1. Happiness and Excitement

#### On Cloud Nine

- **Meaning:** Extremely happy.
- **Example:** "She was on cloud nine after getting the promotion."
- **Usage:** Perfect for describing moments of great joy or satisfaction.

#### Over the Moon

- **Meaning:** Very happy and pleased.
- **Example:** "He was over the moon when he heard the news."
- **Usage:** Often used to describe feelings of elation.

### In Seventh Heaven

- **Meaning:** In a state of extreme happiness.
- **Example:** "They were in seventh heaven after winning the lottery."
- **Usage:** Conveys a sense of bliss and happiness.

### Jump for Joy

- **Meaning:** To be extremely happy and excited.
- **Example:** "She practically jumped for joy when she found out she was accepted into her dream college."
- **Usage:** Often used to describe physical manifestations of happiness.

### Tickled Pink

- **Meaning:** Very pleased and appreciative.
- **Example:** "She was tickled pink by the birthday surprise."
- **Usage:** Used to describe feelings of delight.

## 2. Sadness and Disappointment

### Down in the Dumps

- **Meaning:** Feeling sad or depressed.
- **Example:** "He's been down in the dumps since he lost his job."
- **Usage:** Commonly used to describe feelings of sadness.

**Feel Blue**

- **Meaning:** To feel sad or depressed.
- **Example:** "I always feel blue on rainy days."
- **Usage:** Simple and effective way to express melancholy.

**Heartbroken**

- **Meaning:** Very sad and emotionally upset.
- **Example:** "She was heartbroken when her cat died."
- **Usage:** Often used to describe deep emotional pain, particularly related to loss or disappointment.

**Cry One's Heart Out**

- **Meaning:** To cry a lot and intensely.
- **Example:** "She cried her heart out after the breakup."
- **Usage:** Describes intense emotional crying.

**Beside Oneself**

- **Meaning:** Very upset or distraught.
- **Example:** "He was beside himself when he heard the tragic news."
- **Usage:** Describes a state of extreme emotional distress.

### Down in the Mouth

- **Meaning:** Looking sad or disheartened.
- **Example:** "Why do you look so down in the mouth?"
- **Usage:** Used to describe someone who appears visibly sad.

## 3. Anger and Frustration

### Seeing Red

- **Meaning:** To be very angry.
- **Example:** "He was seeing red when he found out someone had stolen his car."
- **Usage:** Conveys intense anger.

### Blow a Fuse

- **Meaning:** To become very angry.
- **Example:** "She blew a fuse when she saw the mess in the kitchen."
- **Usage:** Often used to describe sudden outbursts of anger.

### Hit the Roof

- **Meaning:** To become extremely angry.
- **Example:** "Dad hit the roof when he saw the dent in the car."
- **Usage:** Commonly used to describe extreme reactions to

anger-inducing situations.

### Bent Out of Shape

- **Meaning:** To be very upset or angry about something.
- **Example:** "Don't get bent out of shape over such a small issue."
- **Usage:** Suggests being disproportionately angry or upset.

### Up in Arms

- **Meaning:** Very angry and ready to fight or argue.
- **Example:** "The community was up in arms over the proposed construction."
- **Usage:** Describes a state of collective anger or agitation.

### Fit to Be Tied

- **Meaning:** Extremely angry.
- **Example:** "He was fit to be tied when he found out about the mistake."
- **Usage:** Describes intense anger.

## 4. Fear and Anxiety

### Shaking Like a Leaf

- **Meaning:** Trembling with fear or anxiety.
- **Example:** "She was shaking like a leaf before her presentation."
- **Usage:** Describes physical manifestations of fear or nervousness.

### Scared to Death

- **Meaning:** Extremely frightened.
- **Example:** "I was scared to death when I heard the loud noise in the middle of the night."
- **Usage:** Hyperbolic expression to convey extreme fear.

### Have Butterflies in One's Stomach

- **Meaning:** To feel nervous or anxious.
- **Example:** "He had butterflies in his stomach before his first date."
- **Usage:** Often used to describe nervous anticipation.

### On Pins and Needles

- **Meaning:** Very anxious or nervous, especially while waiting for something to happen.
- **Example:** "She was on pins and needles waiting for the test results."

- **Usage:** Commonly used to describe nervous waiting.

**Break Out in a Cold Sweat**

- **Meaning:** To become very nervous or frightened.
- **Example:** "I broke out in a cold sweat when I realized I had lost my wallet."
- **Usage:** Describes a physical reaction to fear.

**Quaking in One's Boots**

- **Meaning:** Very scared or nervous.
- **Example:** "He was quaking in his boots before the big presentation."
- **Usage:** Often used to describe visible signs of fear.

## 5. Surprise and Shock

### Jump Out of One's Skin

- **Meaning:** To be extremely surprised or startled.
- **Example:** "I nearly jumped out of my skin when the fire alarm went off."
- **Usage:** Describes a sudden, intense reaction to a surprise.

### Blown Away

- **Meaning:** Extremely impressed or surprised.
- **Example:** "He was blown away by the amazing performance."
- **Usage:** Often used to describe positive surprise or amazement.

### Drop a Bombshell

- **Meaning:** To reveal surprising or shocking news.
- **Example:** "She dropped a bombshell when she announced she was moving to another country."
- **Usage:** Used when delivering unexpected news.

### Take One's Breath Away

- **Meaning:** To be so surprised or impressed that one is momentarily speechless.
- **Example:** "The beautiful view from the top of the mountain took

my breath away."

- **Usage:** Often used to describe overwhelming beauty or awe.

**Mind-Blowing**

- **Meaning:** Very surprising or astonishing.
- **Example:** "The special effects in the movie were mind-blowing."
- **Usage:** Describes something extremely impressive or unexpected.

**Out of the Blue**

- **Meaning:** Suddenly and unexpectedly.
- **Example:** "She called me out of the blue after ten years."
- **Usage:** Used to describe something that happens without warning.

**Practical Tips for Using Emotional Idioms:**

- **Gauge Appropriateness:** Ensure the idiom fits the emotional intensity of the situation. Overstating or understating emotions can lead to misunderstandings.
- **Be Genuine:** Use idioms that genuinely reflect how you feel. Authenticity in expressing emotions strengthens communication.
- **Context Matters:** Some idioms are more suitable for informal contexts, while others can be used in professional settings. Choose accordingly.

## Interactive Exercises

To reinforce your understanding of idioms, here are some interactive exercises. These will help you practice and internalize the idioms covered in this chapter.

## Fill-in-the-Blank Exercises

1. I was __________ when I heard the shocking news. (blown away)
2. After working all night, he decided to __________. (hit the sack)
3. She tried to __________ at the party by telling a joke. (break the ice)
4. We need to get started. Let's __________. (get the ball rolling)
5. He was __________ because he lost his wallet. (down in the dumps)

## Matching Idioms with Meanings

1. On Cloud Nine
    - a. To be very angry
    - b. Extremely happy
    - c. To feel sad
2. Bite Off More Than You Can Chew

- a. To take on too much responsibility
- b. To work late into the night
- c. To be very impressed

3. Shaking Like a Leaf

- a. To be very nervous
- b. To be very happy
- c. To say goodbye

4. Over the Moon

- a. To cry a lot
- b. To be extremely happy
- c. To reveal a secret

5. Blow a Fuse

- a. To become very angry
- b. To be very surprised
- c. To avoid getting to the point

## Writing Prompts

1. Write a short paragraph about a time you were extremely happy. Use at least three idioms from the happiness and excitement section.
2. Describe a situation where you were very nervous or anxious. Incorporate at least two idioms from the fear and anxiety section.
3. Think of a scenario where you had to say goodbye to someone. Use at least three idioms from the goodbyes section to make your narrative more engaging.

## Conversation Starters

1. Imagine you are meeting an old friend after many years. Use idioms from the greetings section to start the conversation.
2. Discuss your weekend plans with a colleague, incorporating idioms related to discussing interests and hobbies.
3. Talk about a recent surprising event in your life using idioms from the surprise and shock section.

## Answers:

To reinforce your understanding of idioms, here are some interactive exercises. These will help you practice and internalize the idioms covered in this chapter.

## Fill-in-the-Blank Exercises

1. I was **blown away** when I heard the shocking news.

2. After working all night, he decided to **hit the sack**.

3. She tried to **break the ice** at the party by telling a joke.

4. We need to get started. Let's **get the ball rolling**.

5. He was **down in the dumps** because he lost his wallet.

## Matching Idioms with Meanings

1. **On Cloud Nine**
    - a. To be very angry
    - **b. Extremely happy**
    - c. To feel sad
2. **Bite Off More Than You Can Chew**
    - **a. To take on too much responsibility**
    - b. To work late into the night
    - c. To be very impressed
3. **Shaking Like a Leaf**
    - **a. To be very nervous**
    - b. To be very happy

- c. To say goodbye

4. **Over the Moon**

   - a. To cry a lot
   - **b. To be extremely happy**
   - c. To reveal a secret

5. **Blow a Fuse**

   - **a. To become very angry**
   - b. To be very surprised
   - c. To avoid getting to the point

## Writing Prompts

1. **Write a short paragraph about a time you were extremely happy. Use at least three idioms from the happiness and excitement section.**

Example:
"When I received the acceptance letter from my dream university, I was
**on cloud nine**
. My parents were
**over the moon**
with pride, and I couldn't help but
**jump for joy**
. It was truly one of the happiest moments of my life."

2. **Describe a situation where you were very nervous or anxious. Incorporate at least two idioms from the fear and anxiety section.**

Example:
"The night before my big presentation, I was
**shaking like a leaf**
. I had
**butterflies in my stomach**
just thinking about standing in front of the entire company. Despite my nerves, I knew I had to face my fears and give it my best shot."

3. **Think of a scenario where you had to say goodbye to someone. Use at least three idioms from the goodbyes section to make your narrative more engaging.**

Example:
"As I prepared to leave for my new job overseas, saying goodbye to my best friend was the hardest part. I told her, 'I'll
**catch you later**
,' even though I knew it might be a while before we saw each other again. She hugged me tightly and said, '
**Take care**
and stay in touch.' I smiled and replied, '
**Until next time**
.'"

## Conversation Starters

1. **Imagine you are meeting an old friend after many years. Use idioms from the greetings section to start the conversation.**

Example:
"Hey,
**long time no see**
!
**What's up**
?
**How's it going**
? It's been ages since we last caught up."

2. **Discuss your weekend plans with a colleague, incorporating idioms related to discussing interests and hobbies.**

Example:
"I'm planning to
**hit the books**
this weekend since I have exams coming up. After that, I might be a bit of a
**couch potato**
and binge-watch some shows. How about you? Any exciting plans?"

3. **Talk about a recent surprising event in your life using idioms from the surprise and shock section.**

Example:
"You won't believe what happened to me last week. I was
**blown away**
when I found out I had won the lottery! It was such a shock that I almost
**jumped out of my skin**
. I'm still trying to
**wrap my head around**
it."

## Fun Facts

**Fun Fact #1: It's Raining Cats and Dogs** The origin of this idiom is uncertain, but one theory suggests it comes from 17th-century England. During heavy rainstorms, the streets would flood, and animals, including cats and dogs, would sometimes be found washed up in the aftermath. The phrase "raining cats and dogs" might have originated from this imagery.

**Fun Fact #2: Break the Ice** This idiom comes from the practice of breaking the ice in frozen rivers to allow ships to pass through. Just as breaking the ice made it possible for ships to navigate, breaking the ice in a conversation makes it easier for people to connect.

**Fun Fact #3: Butterflies in One's Stomach** The sensation of fluttering in the stomach is often experienced when someone is nervous or excited. The idiom "butterflies in one's stomach" perfectly captures this feeling, likening the sensation to the fluttering wings of butterflies.

**Fun Fact #4: Once in a Blue Moon** A "blue moon" refers to the second full moon in a calendar month, which is a rare occurrence. Hence, "once in a blue moon" is used to describe something that happens very infrequently.

**Fun Fact #5: On Cloud Nine** The origin of this idiom is believed to be related to the classification of clouds by the US Weather Bureau, where cloud nine is considered the cumulonimbus cloud, known for its towering, majestic presence. Being "on cloud nine" signifies a high level of happiness, akin to being on top of the world.

By incorporating these idioms into your daily conversations, you can enhance your communication skills and make your speech more engaging and expressive. Remember, the key to mastering idioms is practice and exposure, so don't be afraid to experiment with these phrases in your interactions.

Chapter 3

# Descriptive Idioms

Idioms add color and depth to our language, providing vivid imagery and succinctly conveying complex ideas. In this chapter, we delve into descriptive idioms, focusing on those that characterize people and personalities. Understanding and using these idioms will not only enhance your vocabulary but also help you describe individuals with greater nuance and precision. This chapter is divided into three sections: idioms for people and personalities, idioms for positive traits, and idioms for negative traits. Additionally, we will explore idioms that describe various behaviors.

## Idioms for People and Personalities

People are the heart of any story, and being able to describe them vividly is a valuable skill. Idioms provide a rich resource for adding detail and character to your descriptions. In this section, we will explore a variety of idioms that can be used to depict different types of people and their unique personalities.

## Positive Traits

Describing someone in a positive light can create a favorable impression and highlight their admirable qualities. Here are some idioms that capture positive traits:

### A Diamond in the Rough

- **Meaning:** Someone with exceptional potential or qualities, but who is not yet refined or polished.
- **Example:** "Though he lacks experience, his innovative ideas show he's a diamond in the rough."
- **Usage:** This idiom is often used to describe someone who has inherent qualities that, with some development or training, can shine brightly.

### Salt of the Earth

- **Meaning:** A person who is very kind, reliable, and honest.
- **Example:** "My grandmother is the salt of the earth; she always helps her neighbors."
- **Usage:** This idiom is used to describe someone who is fundamentally good and dependable.

### Heart of Gold

- **Meaning:** A person who is very kind and generous.
- **Example:** "Despite his tough exterior, he has a heart of gold and

would do anything for his friends."

- **Usage:** Often used to describe someone who is inherently kind and compassionate.

**A Class Act**

- **Meaning:** A person who is courteous, dignified, and exhibits excellence.
- **Example:** "Even when she lost, she remained a class act and congratulated the winner."
- **Usage:** Used to highlight someone's grace and poise, especially in challenging situations.

**Good Egg**

- **Meaning:** A good and reliable person.
- **Example:** "You can count on him to help out; he's a good egg."
- **Usage:** This idiom is commonly used to describe someone who is dependable and well-intentioned.

**A Bright Spark**

- **Meaning:** An intelligent and lively person.
- **Example:** "She's a bright spark in the team, always coming up with creative solutions."
- **Usage:** Often used to describe someone who is quick-witted and full of energy.

**An Old Soul**

- **Meaning:** A young person who exhibits wisdom and maturity beyond their years.
- **Example:** "At just ten years old, he's an old soul with a deep understanding of life."
- **Usage:** This idiom is used to highlight a person's mature outlook, regardless of their age.

**Born Leader**

- **Meaning:** Someone who naturally possesses leadership qualities.
- **Example:** "From a young age, she showed she was a born leader, organizing all the neighborhood kids."
- **Usage:** Used to describe someone with innate leadership abilities.

**A Jack of All Trades**

- **Meaning:** A person who is skilled in many different areas.
- **Example:** "He's a jack of all trades; he can fix cars, cook gourmet meals, and play several instruments."
- **Usage:** This idiom highlights versatility and a wide range of skills.

**A Good Sport**

- **Meaning:** Someone who is good-natured and able to take disappointment well.

- **Example:** "Even after losing the game, she was a good sport and congratulated the winners."
- **Usage:** Used to describe someone who maintains a positive attitude, especially in competitive situations.

**A Ray of Sunshine**

- **Meaning:** A person who brings happiness to others.
- **Example:** "Her cheerful demeanor makes her a ray of sunshine in the office."
- **Usage:** This idiom describes someone who consistently brings joy and positivity to those around them.

**Down to Earth**

- **Meaning:** Practical, realistic, and sensible.
- **Example:** "Despite her fame, she remains down to earth and approachable."
- **Usage:** Used to describe someone who is humble and grounded.

**Life of the Party**

- **Meaning:** Someone who is very lively and makes events enjoyable.
- **Example:** "He's always the life of the party, keeping everyone entertained with his stories."
- **Usage:** This idiom is used to describe someone who is fun and energetic in social situations.

## Negative Traits

While positive idioms help us highlight admirable qualities, negative idioms allow us to articulate less favorable characteristics. Here are some idioms that can describe negative traits:

### A Loose Cannon

- **Meaning:** Someone who is unpredictable and can cause trouble if not managed carefully.
- **Example:** "He's a loose cannon in meetings, often derailing the conversation with his outbursts."
- **Usage:** This idiom is used to describe someone whose behavior is erratic and potentially disruptive.

### A Bad Apple

- **Meaning:** A person who negatively influences others.
- **Example:** "One bad apple can spoil the whole team's morale if not addressed."
- **Usage:** This idiom highlights the impact one problematic person can have on a larger group.

### A Wet Blanket

- **Meaning:** A person who dampens others' enthusiasm or fun.
- **Example:** "Don't invite him to the party; he's a wet blanket and always complains."

- **Usage:** Used to describe someone who is negative or unenthusiastic, affecting the mood of others.

### A Tough Nut to Crack

- **Meaning:** Someone who is difficult to deal with or understand.
- **Example:** "Convincing her to change her mind will be a tough nut to crack."
- **Usage:** Often used to describe someone who is stubborn or enigmatic.

### A Cold Fish

- **Meaning:** Someone who is unemotional and distant.
- **Example:** "He might be talented, but he's a cold fish and hard to connect with."
- **Usage:** This idiom is used to describe someone who lacks warmth and is hard to engage with emotionally.

### A Snake in the Grass

- **Meaning:** A deceitful and treacherous person.
- **Example:** "Watch out for him; he's a snake in the grass and can't be trusted."
- **Usage:** Used to describe someone who is secretly dishonest or malicious.

**A Loose Screw**

- **Meaning:** A person who is slightly crazy or eccentric.
- **Example:** "He's got a loose screw, always talking about conspiracy theories."
- **Usage:** This idiom is often used humorously to describe someone with unconventional or odd behavior.

**A Stick in the Mud**

- **Meaning:** Someone who is dull and unadventurous.
- **Example:** "He's such a stick in the mud, never wanting to try anything new."
- **Usage:** Describes someone resistant to change or lacking enthusiasm.

**A Know-It-All**

- **Meaning:** A person who acts as if they know everything.
- **Example:** "Nobody likes working with a know-it-all who never listens to others' ideas."
- **Usage:** Used to describe someone who is overly confident in their knowledge.

**A Backseat Driver**

- **Meaning:** Someone who gives unsolicited advice or directions.

- **Example:** "I can't stand having a backseat driver telling me how to drive."
- **Usage:** Describes someone who interferes with or criticizes others' actions.

**A Fair-Weather Friend**

- **Meaning:** Someone who is only a friend in good times and abandons you in difficult times.
- **Example:** "I realized she was just a fair-weather friend when she disappeared during my tough times."
- **Usage:** Used to describe someone whose loyalty is conditional.

**A Couch Potato**

- **Meaning:** A person who is lazy and inactive.
- **Example:** "He's turned into a real couch potato since he started binge-watching TV shows."
- **Usage:** Describes someone who spends a lot of time sitting or lying down, often watching television.

## Describing Behavior

Describing how someone behaves in different situations can add depth to your characterization. Idioms are particularly useful for painting a vivid picture of behavior. Here are some idioms that describe various types of behavior:

### Go the Extra Mile

- **Meaning:** To make an extra effort to achieve something.
- **Example:** "She always goes the extra mile to ensure her clients are satisfied."
- **Usage:** Used to describe someone who is willing to put in additional effort to accomplish a task.

### Burn the Candle at Both Ends

- **Meaning:** To overwork oneself by doing too many things, especially by staying up late and getting up early.
- **Example:** "He's been burning the candle at both ends preparing for the big presentation."
- **Usage:** This idiom describes someone who is working excessively hard, often at the expense of their well-being.

### Play It by Ear

- **Meaning:** To improvise or decide on the spot, rather than planning ahead.

- **Example:** "We don't have a strict itinerary for the trip; we'll just play it by ear."
- **Usage:** Used to describe a flexible, spontaneous approach to situations.

### Blow Hot and Cold

- **Meaning:** To frequently change one's opinion or attitude.
- **Example:** "He's been blowing hot and cold about joining the new project."
- **Usage:** This idiom describes someone who is inconsistent or fickle.

### Hit the Ground Running

- **Meaning:** To start something energetically and effectively from the very beginning.
- **Example:** "She hit the ground running on her first day at work and impressed everyone."
- **Usage:** Used to describe a strong and enthusiastic start to a new task or role.

### Bite the Bullet

- **Meaning:** To endure a painful or otherwise unpleasant situation that is seen as unavoidable.
- **Example:** "He had to bite the bullet and admit his mistake to the boss."

- **Usage:** Describes facing a difficult situation with courage and determination.

### Jump the Gun

- **Meaning:** To start something too soon, especially without thinking.
- **Example:** "They jumped the gun by announcing the new product before finalizing its design."
- **Usage:** Used to describe premature actions or decisions.

### Keep a Low Profile

- **Meaning:** To avoid attracting attention to oneself.
- **Example:** "After the scandal, he decided to keep a low profile for a while."
- **Usage:** Describes someone who is trying to avoid notice or attention.

### Make Waves

- **Meaning:** To cause trouble or controversy.
- **Example:** "She tends to make waves with her bold opinions."
- **Usage:** This idiom is used to describe someone who disrupts the status quo or stirs up issues.

**Fly Off the Handle**

- **Meaning:** To lose one's temper suddenly and unexpectedly.
- **Example:** "You need to learn to stay calm and not fly off the handle at small issues."
- **Usage:** Describes a sudden and intense reaction of anger.

**Bend Over Backwards**

- **Meaning:** To try very hard to help or please someone.
- **Example:** "She bent over backwards to ensure the guests had everything they needed."
- **Usage:** Used to describe someone making a great effort to be accommodating or helpful.

**Take the Bull by the Horns**

- **Meaning:** To deal with a difficult situation in a very direct or confident way.
- **Example:** "He decided to take the bull by the horns and confront his boss about the issue."
- **Usage:** Describes a proactive and assertive approach to tackling problems.

**Turn a Blind Eye**

- **Meaning:** To ignore something that you know is wrong.

- **Example:** "The manager turned a blind eye to the employee's tardiness."
- **Usage:** Used to describe a deliberate act of ignoring undesirable behavior.

**Jump on the Bandwagon**

- **Meaning:** To join others in doing something that is currently popular or fashionable.
- **Example:** "Everyone is jumping on the bandwagon of the new fitness craze."
- **Usage:** Describes following a trend or popular activity.

**Give Someone the Cold Shoulder**

- **Meaning:** To deliberately ignore someone or treat them in an unfriendly way.
- **Example:** "After their argument, she gave him the cold shoulder for weeks."
- **Usage:** Used to describe intentional social exclusion or unfriendly behavior.

**Spread Like Wildfire**

- **Meaning:** To spread very quickly.
- **Example:** "Rumors about the merger spread like wildfire through the office."

- **Usage:** Describes the rapid dissemination of information, often negative or sensational.

**Throw in the Towel**

- **Meaning:** To give up or admit defeat.
- **Example:** "After several failed attempts, he finally threw in the towel."
- **Usage:** Describes surrendering or ceasing efforts.

**Keep Your Eyes Peeled**

- **Meaning:** To watch carefully for something.
- **Example:** "Keep your eyes peeled for any signs of trouble."
- **Usage:** Used to describe being alert and vigilant.

**Blow One's Own Trumpet**

- **Meaning:** To boast about one's own achievements.
- **Example:** "He's always blowing his own trumpet about his sales records."
- **Usage:** Describes self-promotion or bragging.

**Run in the Family**

- **Meaning:** A characteristic that is common among family members.
- **Example:** "Artistic talent seems to run in their family."

- **Usage:** Used to describe traits or talents that appear frequently within a family lineage.

### To Beat Around the Bush

- **Meaning:** To avoid talking about the main topic.
- **Example:** "Stop beating around the bush and tell me what you really think."
- **Usage:** Describes someone who is indirect or evasive.

### To Bite Off More Than You Can Chew

- **Meaning:** To take on more than you can handle.
- **Example:** "He bit off more than he could chew by accepting three major projects at once."
- **Usage:** Describes someone who overestimates their ability to manage tasks.

### To Cry Over Spilled Milk

- **Meaning:** To lament something that cannot be changed.
- **Example:** "There's no use crying over spilled milk; we just have to move on."
- **Usage:** Used to advise against wasting time on regrets.

### To Bark Up the Wrong Tree

- **Meaning:** To make a mistake or pursue the wrong course of action.

- **Example:** "If you think I'm responsible, you're barking up the wrong tree."
- **Usage:** Describes someone who is misguided or wrong in their assumptions.

**To Blow One's Top**

- **Meaning:** To become extremely angry.
- **Example:** "He blew his top when he found out someone had scratched his car."
- **Usage:** Describes a sudden, intense outburst of anger.

**To Call It a Day**

- **Meaning:** To stop working for the day.
- **Example:** "We've done enough work; let's call it a day."
- **Usage:** Used to indicate the end of a period of work or activity.

**To Keep One's Nose to the Grindstone**

- **Meaning:** To work hard and continuously.
- **Example:** "She kept her nose to the grindstone and finished the project ahead of schedule."
- **Usage:** Describes a strong work ethic and diligence.

**To Pull Someone's Leg**

- **Meaning:** To tease or joke with someone.
- **Example:** "Relax, I'm just pulling your leg about the new rules."
- **Usage:** Describes playful teasing.

**To Cut Corners**

- **Meaning:** To do something in the easiest or most inexpensive way, often compromising quality.
- **Example:** "The contractor cut corners on the building materials, leading to problems later."
- **Usage:** Describes taking shortcuts that can lead to inferior results.

**To Jump Through Hoops**

- **Meaning:** To go through many difficult procedures to achieve something.
- **Example:** "I had to jump through hoops to get my visa approved."
- **Usage:** Describes a complicated and arduous process.

**To Keep One's Cool**

- **Meaning:** To stay calm in a difficult situation.
- **Example:** "Despite the chaos, she kept her cool and handled the situation efficiently."

- **Usage:** Describes maintaining composure under stress.

**To Hit the Books**

- **Meaning:** To study very hard.
- **Example:** "She hit the books all weekend to prepare for her exams."
- **Usage:** Describes intense study efforts.

**To Face the Music**

- **Meaning:** To accept the consequences of one's actions.
- **Example:** "After his mistake, he had to face the music and apologize."
- **Usage:** Describes taking responsibility for one's actions.

**To Bend the Rules**

- **Meaning:** To slightly break or alter the rules.
- **Example:** "He bent the rules to allow his friend to enter the competition late."
- **Usage:** Describes minor rule-breaking often seen as justifiable.

**To Let the Cat Out of the Bag**

- **Meaning:** To reveal a secret, often unintentionally.
- **Example:** "She let the cat out of the bag about the surprise party."
- **Usage:** Describes the accidental disclosure of information.

### To Spill the Beans

- **Meaning:** To reveal confidential information.
- **Example:** "He spilled the beans about the merger before it was officially announced."
- **Usage:** Used to describe the act of disclosing secrets.

### To Turn Over a New Leaf

- **Meaning:** To start behaving in a better or more responsible way.
- **Example:** "After the scandal, he promised to turn over a new leaf."
- **Usage:** Describes making a significant change in one's behavior.

### To Get Cold Feet

- **Meaning:** To become nervous or hesitant about a major decision.
- **Example:** "She got cold feet just before the wedding and called it off."
- **Usage:** Describes last-minute doubts or fears.

## Practical Tips for Using Descriptive Idioms

**Context is Key:** Ensure that the idiom you choose fits the context of the conversation. Some idioms may be too informal or specific for certain situations.

**Know Your Audience:** Tailor your language to the understanding and cultural background of your audience. Some idioms may not translate well or could be misinterpreted.

**Practice:** Regular use of idioms in your speech or writing will help you become more comfortable with them. Listening to native speakers and reading widely can provide examples of idioms in context.

**Mix Idioms with Plain Language:** Overuse of idioms can make your language sound forced or overly embellished. Balance idiomatic expressions with straightforward language to maintain clarity.

**Learn the Nuances:** Some idioms have subtle connotations or historical contexts that can add depth to their meaning. Understanding these nuances can enhance your use of idioms.

## Fun Facts

**Fun Fact #1: A Diamond in the Rough** The phrase "a diamond in the rough" dates back to the 17th century and refers to an unpolished diamond that has great potential value but needs refinement. This idiom highlights the idea that valuable qualities can be found beneath a rough exterior.

**Fun Fact #2: Salt of the Earth** This idiom has biblical origins, specifically from the Sermon on the Mount in the Gospel of Matthew. Jesus referred to his followers as the "salt of the earth," implying they were of great value and importance. Today, it describes someone who is fundamentally good and honest.

**Fun Fact #3: Blow Hot and Cold** This idiom comes from Aesop's fable "The Man and the Satyr," where a man blows on his hands to warm them and blows on his soup to cool it. The satyr accuses him of being inconsistent. The phrase now describes someone who frequently changes their opinions or behavior.

**Fun Fact #4: Bite the Bullet** In the past, during times of war or without anesthesia, soldiers would bite on a bullet to endure pain during surgery or amputation. This idiom now means to face a difficult situation with courage.

**Fun Fact #5: Throw in the Towel** This idiom originates from boxing, where a trainer throws a towel into the ring to signal that their fighter can no longer continue. It now means to give up or admit defeat.

By incorporating these idioms into your daily conversations, you can add color and depth to your descriptions of people and their behaviors. Practice and exposure are key to mastering idioms, so don't hesitate to use them in your interactions and observe how native speakers use them. As you become more comfortable with these expressions, your ability to communicate effectively and expressively will grow, making your language more engaging and dynamic.

Chapter 4

# Action Idioms

Idioms add dynamism and flair to our language, often encapsulating complex ideas in a few words. They are particularly useful when discussing activities and processes, as they provide a vivid and memorable way to describe actions and situations. In this chapter, we focus on action idioms, specifically those related to work and study. Understanding these idioms will enhance your ability to communicate effectively in both professional and academic settings. This chapter is divided into sections on workplace phrases and academic phrases, followed by real-life case studies and practice dialogues to help you master these idioms.

## Idioms About Work and Study

### Workplace Phrases

The workplace is a dynamic environment where communication needs to be clear and efficient. Idioms play a significant role in achieving this, adding color to conversations and helping to convey complex ideas succinctly. Here are some commonly used idioms in the workplace:

**1. Burn the Midnight Oil**

- **Meaning:** To work late into the night.
- **Example:** "With the deadline approaching, we had to burn the midnight oil to finish the project."
- **Usage:** This idiom is often used to describe situations where extra effort is required to meet a deadline or complete a task.

**2. Hit the Ground Running**

- **Meaning:** To start a task or project with a lot of energy and enthusiasm.
- **Example:** "When she joined the company, she hit the ground running and quickly became a valuable team member."
- **Usage:** Used to describe someone who starts something energetically and effectively right from the beginning.

**3. Keep One's Nose to the Grindstone**

- **Meaning:** To work hard and continuously.
- **Example:** "If you keep your nose to the grindstone, you'll finish the report by the end of the day."
- **Usage:** This idiom emphasizes the importance of hard work and dedication.

**4. Climb the Corporate Ladder**

- **Meaning:** To advance in one's career, typically through promotions.

- **Example:** "She's been working hard to climb the corporate ladder and now she's a senior manager."
- **Usage:** Often used to describe career progression and ambition.

**5. Pull Your Weight**

- **Meaning:** To do your fair share of the work.
- **Example:** "Everyone needs to pull their weight if we want to complete this project on time."
- **Usage:** This idiom is used to encourage team members to contribute equally to a task.

**6. Cut Corners**

- **Meaning:** To do something in the easiest or cheapest way, often sacrificing quality.
- **Example:** "If we cut corners on this project, it could lead to bigger problems later on."
- **Usage:** Used to caution against compromising quality for the sake of convenience.

**7. Go the Extra Mile**

- **Meaning:** To make an extra effort beyond what is expected.
- **Example:** "She's always willing to go the extra mile to ensure her clients are satisfied."

- **Usage:** This idiom is used to describe someone who exceeds expectations in their work.

**8. Learn the Ropes**

- **Meaning:** To learn how to do a particular job or task.
- **Example:** "It took a few weeks, but I've finally learned the ropes of my new position."
- **Usage:** Commonly used when someone is new to a job or role and is in the process of learning how to perform their duties.

**9. By the Book**

- **Meaning:** To do things according to the rules or the official way.
- **Example:** "The new manager insists that everything be done by the book."
- **Usage:** This idiom is often used to emphasize strict adherence to rules or procedures.

**10. On the Same Page**

- **Meaning:** To have a shared understanding or agreement about something.
- **Example:** "Let's have a meeting to ensure we're all on the same page before we proceed."
- **Usage:** Used to emphasize the importance of alignment and mutual understanding within a team.

### 11. Raise the Bar

- **Meaning:** To set a higher standard of quality or performance.
- **Example:** "Our recent success has raised the bar for future projects."
- **Usage:** This idiom is used to describe an increase in expectations or standards.

### 12. Back to the Drawing Board

- **Meaning:** To start over, often because a previous attempt failed.
- **Example:** "The client rejected our proposal, so it's back to the drawing board."
- **Usage:** Commonly used when a project or plan needs to be reconsidered from the beginning.

### 13. Break the Ice

- **Meaning:** To initiate conversation in a social setting, making people feel more comfortable.
- **Example:** "She told a funny story to break the ice at the beginning of the meeting."
- **Usage:** Often used in the context of starting conversations or easing initial awkwardness.

### 14. Touch Base

- **Meaning:** To briefly make contact with someone.

- **Example:** "I'll touch base with you next week to see how the project is going."
- **Usage:** Often used in business contexts to suggest checking in with someone.

**15. Think Outside the Box**

- **Meaning:** To think creatively and unconventionally.
- **Example:** "We'll need to think outside the box to come up with a solution to this problem."
- **Usage:** This idiom encourages innovative and non-traditional thinking.

## Academic Phrases

The academic world is rich with idioms that describe various aspects of studying, learning, and intellectual endeavors. These idioms are useful for students, teachers, and anyone involved in education. Here are some commonly used academic idioms:

**1. Hit the Books**

- **Meaning:** To study very hard.
- **Example:** "I've got exams next week, so it's time to hit the books."
- **Usage:** This idiom is commonly used among students or when discussing academic efforts.

**2. Pull an All-Nighter**

- **Meaning:** To stay up all night working on a task, usually studying.
- **Example:** "I had to pull an all-nighter to finish my term paper on time."
- **Usage:** Often used by students during exam periods or when facing tight deadlines.

**3. Burn the Midnight Oil**

- **Meaning:** To work late into the night.
- **Example:** "She burned the midnight oil preparing for her final exams."
- **Usage:** This idiom describes the effort of working late hours to complete tasks.

**4. Make the Grade**

- **Meaning:** To reach the necessary standard; to succeed.
- **Example:** "If you study hard, you'll make the grade."
- **Usage:** Often used to describe academic success or meeting specific standards.

**5. Learn by Heart**

- **Meaning:** To memorize something completely.
- **Example:** "You need to learn these formulas by heart for the test."

- **Usage:** This idiom emphasizes the importance of memorization.

**6. Pass with Flying Colors**

- **Meaning:** To pass a test or complete something successfully with high marks.
- **Example:** "She passed her entrance exam with flying colors."
- **Usage:** Used to describe exceptional success or achievement.

**7. Drop the Ball**

- **Meaning:** To make a mistake or fail to do something important.
- **Example:** "I really dropped the ball by forgetting to submit my assignment on time."
- **Usage:** This idiom is used to acknowledge a failure or oversight.

**8. A for Effort**

- **Meaning:** To recognize someone's hard work even if they did not succeed.
- **Example:** "He didn't win the competition, but he gets an A for effort."
- **Usage:** Used to praise someone for their hard work and determination.

**9. Get One's Act Together**

- **Meaning:** To start organizing oneself to accomplish something.

- **Example:** "You need to get your act together if you want to graduate on time."
- **Usage:** This idiom encourages someone to become more organized and focused.

**10. Brainstorm**

- **Meaning:** To generate many ideas quickly.
- **Example:** "Let's brainstorm some ideas for our group project."
- **Usage:** Often used in academic and professional settings to encourage creative thinking.

**11. Cut Class**

- **Meaning:** To skip a class or not attend.
- **Example:** "He often cuts class to hang out with his friends."
- **Usage:** This idiom describes the act of intentionally missing a class.

**12. Eager Beaver**

- **Meaning:** A person who is enthusiastic and works very hard.
- **Example:** "She's always the first to arrive and the last to leave; she's a real eager beaver."
- **Usage:** Used to describe someone who is very diligent and hardworking.

**13. Call the Shots**

- **Meaning:** To be in control and make decisions.
- **Example:** "As the team leader, she calls the shots."
- **Usage:** This idiom is used to describe someone who has authority and makes important decisions.

**14. To Cram**

- **Meaning:** To study intensively over a short period of time just before an exam.
- **Example:** "I had to cram for my history test last night."
- **Usage:** Often used by students who prepare for exams at the last minute.

**15. Bookworm**

- **Meaning:** A person who enjoys reading and spends a lot of time doing it.
- **Example:** "She's a bookworm, always reading in the library."
- **Usage:** This idiom describes someone who loves reading and is often found with a book.

## Case Studies and Examples

To understand how these idioms are used in real-life scenarios, let's explore some detailed case studies and examples. These will provide context and illustrate how idioms can be seamlessly integrated into conversations and written communication.

## Case Study 1: A Busy Week at the Office

**Scenario:** Jane is a project manager at a tech company. Her team is working on a major software update, and the deadline is approaching fast.

**Dialogue:**

- **Jane:** "Alright team, we need to burn the midnight oil this week if we want to meet our deadline."
- **Tom:** "No problem, Jane. I've already hit the ground running with the new code module."
- **Sarah:** "I'll make sure we don't cut corners with the testing phase."
- **Jane:** "Great. Remember, everyone needs to pull their weight. Let's aim to exceed expectations and go the extra mile."

**Analysis:** In this scenario, Jane uses idioms like "burn the midnight oil," "hit the ground running," "cut corners," "pull their weight," and "go the extra mile" to motivate her team and emphasize the importance of their efforts.

## Case Study 2: Preparing for Finals

**Scenario:** Mike is a college student facing final exams. He has a lot of material to cover and limited time.

**Dialogue:**

- **Mike:** "I've got so much to study. Looks like I'll have to pull an all-nighter."

- **Jenny:** "Don't forget to hit the books for your biology exam."
- **Mike:** "Yeah, I've already started burning the midnight oil. I need to make the grade this semester."
- **Jenny:** "You can do it. Just learn the key concepts by heart and you'll pass with flying colors."

**Analysis:** Mike and Jenny use idioms like "pull an all-nighter," "hit the books," "burn the midnight oil," "make the grade," "learn by heart," and "pass with flying colors" to discuss their study strategies and academic goals.

## Case Study 3: Launching a New Product

**Scenario:** The marketing team at a startup is preparing for the launch of their new app. They need to ensure everything is perfect before the launch date.

**Dialogue:**

- **Alice:** "We've got to get our act together before the launch next week."
- **Ben:** "Agreed. Let's brainstorm some final ideas for the campaign."
- **Carol:** "I'll touch base with the developers to make sure we're all on the same page."
- **Dave:** "We need to raise the bar with this launch to outshine our competitors."
- **Alice:** "Absolutely. If anything goes wrong, it's back to the drawing

board."

**Analysis:** In this scenario, Alice, Ben, Carol, and Dave use idioms like "get our act together," "brainstorm," "touch base," "on the same page," "raise the bar," and "back to the drawing board" to coordinate their efforts and set high standards for the product launch.

## Practice Dialogues

Practice makes perfect, and using idioms in conversation helps reinforce their meanings and appropriate usage. Here are some sample dialogues incorporating the idioms discussed in this chapter:

### Dialogue 1: Discussing Workload

**Characters:** Emily and Jake are colleagues at a marketing firm.

**Emily:** "Hey Jake, how's the new campaign coming along?" **Jake:** "It's a lot of work, but I'm keeping my nose to the grindstone." **Emily:** "That's great to hear. Just make sure you don't burn the candle at both ends." **Jake:** "I know, I know. I'm trying to go the extra mile without cutting corners." **Emily:** "If you need any help, just let me know. We all need to pull our weight to meet the deadline." **Jake:** "Thanks, Emily. I'll definitely touch base if I need anything."

**Analysis:** In this dialogue, Emily and Jake use idioms like "keeping my nose to the grindstone," "burn the candle at both ends," "go the extra mile," "cutting corners," "pull our weight," and "touch base" to discuss their work and offer support.

### Dialogue 2: Study Session

**Characters:** Rachel and Tom are college students preparing for their final exams.

**Rachel:** "Hey Tom, are you ready for the math exam tomorrow?" **Tom:** "Not really. I had to cram all night." **Rachel:** "Me too. I hit the books right after dinner." **Tom:** "I just hope I make the grade. This semester has been tough." **Rachel:** "You'll be fine. Just remember to learn the formulas by heart." **Tom:** "Thanks, Rachel. Good luck! Let's pass with flying colors."

**Analysis:** Rachel and Tom use idioms like "cram all night," "hit the books," "make the grade," "learn the formulas by heart," and "pass with flying colors" to express their study efforts and wish each other luck.

## Dialogue 3: Project Planning

**Characters:** Karen and Steve are part of a team planning a new project.

**Karen:** "Steve, do you have a moment to brainstorm ideas for the new project?" **Steve:** "Sure, Karen. Let's think outside the box this time." **Karen:** "Good idea. We need to raise the bar and come up with something innovative." **Steve:** "Agreed. We should also ensure we're on the same page with the rest of the team." **Karen:** "Absolutely. I'll send an email to touch base with everyone." **Steve:** "Great. If anything doesn't work, we can always go back to the drawing board."

**Analysis:** In this dialogue, Karen and Steve use idioms like "brainstorm," "think outside the box," "raise the bar," "on the same page," "touch base," and "back to the drawing board" to discuss their project planning process.

## Real-Life Scenarios Using Idioms

To further illustrate the use of idioms in work and study contexts, let's examine some detailed real-life scenarios.

## Scenario 1: A Product Launch

**Background:** Tech Innovators Inc. is launching a new gadget. The marketing and development teams are under pressure to ensure everything goes smoothly.

**Meeting Transcript:**

- **CEO:** "Alright team, we need to hit the ground running with this launch. There's no room for error."
- **Marketing Head:** "We've already started brainstorming campaign ideas. We'll make sure to think outside the box."
- **Development Head:** "We're burning the midnight oil to fix the last few bugs. Quality is our top priority; we won't cut corners."
- **Sales Head:** "I'll touch base with our major clients to keep them in the loop and ensure we're all on the same page."
- **CEO:** "Perfect. Let's aim to raise the bar and set a new standard in the industry. If anything goes wrong, we'll go back to the drawing board."

**Analysis:** In this scenario, various idioms are used to emphasize the urgency, creativity, hard work, and coordination required for the product launch. The CEO and team members use idioms like "hit the ground running," "brainstorming," "think outside the box," "burning the midnight oil," "cut corners," "touch base," "on the same page," "raise the bar," and "back to the drawing board" to convey their plans and expectations.

## Scenario 2: Preparing for an Important Exam

**Background:** Lisa is a university student preparing for her final exams. She has a lot of material to cover and is feeling stressed.

**Study Plan Discussion:**

- **Lisa:** "I have to pull an all-nighter tonight to review all my notes."
- **Friend:** "Make sure you hit the books on the key topics. Don't just skim through."
- **Lisa:** "I know. I've been burning the midnight oil all week. I need to make the grade in this exam."
- **Friend:** "You'll do fine. Just learn the key concepts by heart and practice solving problems."
- **Lisa:** "Thanks. I hope to pass with flying colors. I've put in a lot of effort."
- **Friend:** "You've got this. Just stay focused and don't drop the ball."

**Analysis:** Lisa and her friend use idioms like "pull an all-nighter," "hit the books," "burning the midnight oil," "make the grade," "learn by heart," "pass with flying colors," and "drop the ball" to discuss her study strategies and offer encouragement.

## Scenario 3: Office Team Building

**Background:** The management at Creative Solutions is organizing a team-building workshop to improve collaboration and productivity among employees.

**Workshop Transcript:**

- **Facilitator:** "Welcome everyone! Today, we'll start with some icebreaker activities to break the ice."
- **Team Member 1:** "I always enjoy these sessions. It's a great way to get on the same page with colleagues."
- **Team Member 2:** "Yes, and it helps us learn the ropes, especially for new employees."
- **Facilitator:** "Exactly. We'll brainstorm ideas on how to improve our processes and raise the bar for our projects."
- **Team Member 3:** "I think this will help us hit the ground running on our upcoming assignments."
- **Facilitator:** "That's the spirit! Remember, our goal is to think outside the box and come up with innovative solutions."

**Analysis:** During the workshop, the facilitator and team members use idioms like "break the ice," "get on the same page," "learn the ropes," "brainstorm," "raise the bar," "hit the ground running," and "think outside the box" to emphasize the importance of team building, learning, and creativity.

## Practice Exercises

To reinforce your understanding of these idioms, here are some practice exercises. Try to complete these exercises to test your knowledge and see how well you can apply the idioms in various contexts.

**Exercise 1: Fill in the Blanks**

1. With the deadline approaching, we had to ________ to finish the project. (burn the midnight oil)
2. She joined the company and ________, quickly becoming a valuable team member. (hit the ground running)
3. Everyone needs to ________ if we want to complete this project on time. (pull their weight)
4. Let's ________ some ideas for our group project. (brainstorm)
5. To succeed in this course, you need to ________ and study hard. (hit the books)
6. After several failed attempts, he finally ________. (threw in the towel)

**Exercise 2: Matching Idioms with Meanings**

1. Learn the ropes
    - a. To ignore something wrong
    - b. To learn how to do a job or task
    - c. To work late into the night
2. Raise the bar

- a. To set a higher standard
- b. To pull one's weight
- c. To think creatively

3. Pull an all-nighter
   - a. To work hard continuously
   - b. To stay up all night working
   - c. To get on the same page
4. Touch base
   - a. To make contact briefly
   - b. To cut corners
   - c. To brainstorm

**Exercise 3: Writing Prompts**

1. Write a short paragraph about a time you had to work hard to meet a deadline. Use at least three idioms from the workplace phrases section.

2. Describe a study session before a big exam. Incorporate at least three idioms from the academic phrases section.

3. Think of a scenario where your team had to start over on a project. Use at least three idioms from the workplace phrases section to make your narrative more engaging.

**Exercise 4: Conversation Starters**

1. Imagine you are discussing a new project with a colleague. Use idioms from the workplace phrases section to start the conversation.
2. Talk about your study plans for an upcoming exam with a friend, incorporating idioms related to academic efforts.
3. Discuss a recent team-building activity with your team members using idioms from the workplace phrases section.

By mastering these action idioms related to work and study, you can enhance your communication skills in professional and academic settings. These idioms not only make your language more vivid and engaging but also help you convey complex ideas succinctly. Practice using these idioms in real-life situations, and pay attention to how native speakers incorporate them into their conversations. As you become more comfortable with these expressions, your ability to communicate effectively and expressively will grow, making your language more dynamic and impactful.

## Answers:

1. **Fill in the Blanks**
2. burn the midnight oil
3. hit the ground running
4. pull their weight
5. brainstorm

6. hit the books

7. threw in the towel

**Multiple Choice**

1. b (Learn the ropes)

2. a (Raise the bar)

3. b (Pull an all-nighter)

4. a (Touch base)

# Chapter 5
# Fun and Playful Idioms

Idioms related to fun and play bring a light-hearted and engaging element to language. They are often derived from sports, games, and other recreational activities, capturing the competitive spirit and enjoyment associated with these pursuits. This section explores idioms about sports and games, focusing on themes of winning and losing, playing and competing, and includes quizzes and games to make learning these idioms enjoyable.

## Idioms About Sports and Games

## Winning and Losing

In the realm of sports and games, winning and losing are two fundamental outcomes that inspire a wide range of idioms. These expressions not only capture the essence of competition but also offer valuable life lessons about perseverance, humility, and resilience. Here are some common idioms related to winning and losing:

### Win Hands Down

- **Meaning:** To win easily or decisively.

- **Example:** "She won the chess tournament hands down, defeating all her opponents effortlessly."
- **Usage:** This idiom is used to describe a victory that is achieved with little difficulty, emphasizing the ease and decisiveness of the win.

**Throw in the Towel**

- **Meaning:** To give up or admit defeat.
- **Example:** "After losing the first three rounds, the team decided to throw in the towel."
- **Usage:** Often used in sports and competitive contexts, this idiom signifies surrendering or conceding defeat.

**Come Up Short**

- **Meaning:** To fail to reach a goal or to lose by a small margin.
- **Example:** "Despite their best efforts, they came up short in the final minutes of the game."
- **Usage:** This idiom describes situations where someone almost succeeds but ultimately falls short of their objective.

**Go for the Gold**

- **Meaning:** To aim for the best or to strive for the highest achievement.
- **Example:** "She trained rigorously, determined to go for the gold at the Olympics."

- **Usage:** Derived from the concept of winning a gold medal, this idiom encourages striving for excellence.

### 5. Down for the Count

- **Meaning:** Defeated, incapacitated, or unable to continue.
- **Example:** "After the heavy blow, the boxer was down for the count and couldn't get up."
- **Usage:** This idiom, originating from boxing, describes someone who is defeated or temporarily out of action.

### 6. Take the Lead

- **Meaning:** To assume control or become the front-runner in a competition.
- **Example:** "The marathon runner took the lead in the final mile and won the race."
- **Usage:** Used in competitive scenarios, this idiom highlights someone taking a dominant position.

### 7. Neck and Neck

- **Meaning:** Very close in a competition, with neither side having a clear advantage.
- **Example:** "The two candidates were neck and neck in the polls leading up to the election."
- **Usage:** Often used to describe closely contested races or

competitions.

**8. Hit a Home Run**

- **Meaning:** To achieve great success.
- **Example:** "Her presentation hit a home run with the audience, earning her high praise."
- **Usage:** Borrowed from baseball, this idiom signifies outstanding achievement.

**9. Take It on the Chin**

- **Meaning:** To accept a difficult situation or setback with courage and resilience.
- **Example:** "Despite the loss, the team took it on the chin and vowed to come back stronger."
- **Usage:** This idiom emphasizes accepting defeat gracefully and with determination.

**10. Pull Off an Upset**

- **Meaning:** To win unexpectedly against a favored opponent.
- **Example:** "The underdog team pulled off an upset by defeating the reigning champions."
- **Usage:** Used to describe surprising victories, particularly when the winner was not expected to succeed.

**11. Come Out on Top**

- **Meaning:** To win or be the best in a competition.
- **Example:** "Despite the tough competition, she came out on top."
- **Usage:** This idiom is used to describe someone who emerges as the winner in a challenging situation.

**12. Beat the Clock**

- **Meaning:** To finish something before the time limit expires.
- **Example:** "They managed to beat the clock and submit their project just in time."
- **Usage:** Often used to describe completing tasks or goals within a deadline.

**13. In the Running**

- **Meaning:** Having a chance to win or succeed.
- **Example:** "He's still in the running for the promotion despite the tough competition."
- **Usage:** Used to describe someone who is a contender in a competition or for an opportunity.

**14. Come from Behind**

- **Meaning:** To win after being behind in a competition.
- **Example:** "The team came from behind to win the championship in the last minute."

- **Usage:** Describes a situation where someone wins despite initially being at a disadvantage.

**15. On a Losing Streak**

- **Meaning:** Experiencing a series of losses or failures.
- **Example:** "The team is on a losing streak, having lost their last five games."
- **Usage:** Used to describe a continuous series of unsuccessful outcomes.

## Playing and Competing

Playing and competing are integral aspects of sports and games, fostering camaraderie, skill development, and healthy rivalry. Idioms in this category reflect the strategies, tactics, and experiences associated with engaging in various forms of play. Here are some idioms that capture the spirit of playing and competing:

**1. Call the Shots**

- **Meaning:** To be in control and make important decisions.
- **Example:** "As the team captain, she calls the shots during the game."
- **Usage:** This idiom highlights authority and decision-making power, often used in sports contexts.

**2. Play Hardball**

- **Meaning:** To act aggressively and ruthlessly to achieve one's goals.

- **Example:** "Negotiations got tough, but they decided to play hardball to secure a better deal."
- **Usage:** Originating from baseball, this idiom is used in competitive situations where assertiveness is required.

**3. Level Playing Field**

- **Meaning:** A situation where everyone has an equal chance of success.
- **Example:** "The new regulations aim to create a level playing field for all competitors."
- **Usage:** This idiom is often used to describe fair competition without any advantages or disadvantages.

**4. Drop the Ball**

- **Meaning:** To make a mistake or fail to do something important.
- **Example:** "The marketing team dropped the ball by missing the campaign deadline."
- **Usage:** Commonly used to describe errors or oversights, particularly in competitive or high-stakes situations.

**5. The Ball Is in Your Court**

- **Meaning:** It is your turn to take action or make a decision.
- **Example:** "I've made my offer, so now the ball is in your court."
- **Usage:** This idiom emphasizes responsibility and the need for

action from the other party.

**6. Play Your Cards Right**

- **Meaning:** To make strategic decisions that maximize one's chances of success.
- **Example:** "If you play your cards right, you could land that promotion."
- **Usage:** Borrowed from card games, this idiom highlights the importance of strategy and careful planning.

**7. Take a Rain Check**

- **Meaning:** To decline an invitation or offer but suggest that it may be accepted at a later time.
- **Example:** "I can't join you for dinner tonight, but can I take a rain check?"
- **Usage:** Often used to politely postpone participation or acceptance.

**8. Throw Your Hat in the Ring**

- **Meaning:** To announce one's intention to compete or participate.
- **Example:** "Several candidates have thrown their hats in the ring for the presidency."
- **Usage:** This idiom is used to indicate entering a competition or contest.

**9. Par for the Course**

- **Meaning:** Typical or expected behavior in a given situation.
- **Example:** "Delays are par for the course when dealing with government agencies."
- **Usage:** Originating from golf, this idiom describes something that is normal or expected.

**10. Ahead of the Game**

- **Meaning:** To be more advanced or successful than others.
- **Example:** "By adopting new technologies early, the company stays ahead of the game."
- **Usage:** This idiom emphasizes being proactive and staying competitive.

**11. Game Plan**

- **Meaning:** A strategy or plan for achieving success.
- **Example:** "The coach outlined the game plan for the upcoming match."
- **Usage:** Commonly used in sports and business to describe a strategic approach.

**12. Keep Your Eye on the Ball**

- **Meaning:** To stay focused on the main goal or objective.
- **Example:** "Despite the distractions, she kept her eye on the ball and finished the project."

- **Usage:** This idiom underscores the importance of maintaining focus.

**13. Give It Your Best Shot**

- **Meaning:** To try as hard as possible.
- **Example:** "Even if you don't win, just give it your best shot."
- **Usage:** Encourages maximum effort and determination.

**14. In the Ballpark**

- **Meaning:** Approximately correct or within a reasonable range.
- **Example:** "The cost estimate is in the ballpark of $10,000."
- **Usage:** This idiom is used to describe estimates or guesses that are reasonably accurate.

**15. Out of Left Field**

- **Meaning:** Unexpected or surprising.
- **Example:** "Her suggestion came out of left field, but it was a good idea."
- **Usage:** This idiom is used to describe something that is surprising or unusual.

**16. Jump on the Bandwagon**

- **Meaning:** To join others in doing something that is currently popular.

- **Example:** "Many companies are jumping on the bandwagon of green technology."
- **Usage:** Describes following a trend or popular movement.

**17. Roll with the Punches**

- **Meaning:** To adapt to difficult circumstances.
- **Example:** "In this industry, you need to roll with the punches and be ready for anything."
- **Usage:** Emphasizes the importance of resilience and adaptability.

**18. Know the Ropes**

- **Meaning:** To be familiar with the details of a job or situation.
- **Example:** "It took a while, but now I know the ropes at my new job."
- **Usage:** Used to describe understanding the intricacies of a task or environment.

**19. Show One's Hand**

- **Meaning:** To reveal one's intentions or plans.
- **Example:** "He was careful not to show his hand too early in the negotiation."
- **Usage:** This idiom, derived from card games, emphasizes strategic concealment.

### 20. Two Strikes Against

- **Meaning:** Being in a difficult or disadvantageous situation.
- **Example:** "With two strikes against them, the team needs to perform exceptionally well to win."
- **Usage:** Describes facing significant challenges or setbacks.

## Quizzes and Games

To make learning these idioms fun and engaging, let's incorporate some quizzes and games. These activities will help reinforce your understanding and retention of the idioms discussed in this chapter.

## Practice Dialogues

Practicing idioms in conversation helps to solidify their meanings and appropriate usage. Here are some sample dialogues incorporating the idioms discussed:

## Dialogue 1: Office Strategy Meeting

**Characters:** Mark and Lisa are discussing their strategy for an upcoming project at their company.

**Mark:** "Alright, Lisa, what's our game plan for this project?"

**Lisa:** "I think we should start by brainstorming ideas. We need to think outside the box to come up with something innovative."

**Mark:** "Good idea. Let's also ensure we're on the same page with the rest of the team."

**Lisa:** "Absolutely. We can't afford to drop the ball on this one."

**Mark:** "Agreed. We'll go the extra mile to make sure everything is perfect."

**Lisa:** "And if anything goes wrong, we'll be ready to go back to the drawing board."

**Analysis:** In this dialogue, Mark and Lisa use idioms like "game plan," "brainstorming," "think outside the box," "on the same page," "drop the ball," "go the extra mile," and "back to the drawing board" to discuss their project strategy and contingency plans.

## Dialogue 2: Competitive Sports Team

**Characters:** Coach John and his basketball team are discussing their strategy for the upcoming championship game.

**Coach John:** "Team, we've got a tough game ahead of us. We need to hit the ground running from the start."

**Player 1:** "Coach, should we play hardball with their top players?"

**Coach John:** "Absolutely. We'll call the shots on defense and make sure to keep our eye on the ball."

**Player 2:** "What if we fall behind?"

**Coach John:** "Stay focused and give it your best shot. Remember, we can pull off an upset if we play smart."

**Player 1:** "Got it, Coach. We'll go for the gold!"

**Analysis:** In this dialogue, Coach John and his players use idioms like "hit the ground running," "play hardball," "call the shots," "keep our eye on the ball," "give it your best shot," "pull off an upset," and "go for the gold" to discuss their game strategy and motivation.

## Dialogue 3: Study Group Session

**Characters:** Emma, Jack, and Lily are part of a study group preparing for their final exams.

**Emma:** "Alright, everyone, let's hit the books and make the most of this study session."

**Jack:** "I agree. We need to pull an all-nighter to cover all the material."

**Lily:** "Don't forget to learn the key concepts by heart. That's crucial for the exam."

**Emma:** "And let's not get distracted. We need to keep our eye on the ball."

**Jack:** "If we do this right, we'll pass with flying colors."

**Analysis:** In this dialogue, Emma, Jack, and Lily use idioms like "hit the books," "pull an all-nighter," "learn by heart," "keep our eye on the ball," and "pass with flying colors" to emphasize their study efforts and goals.

## Dialogue 4: Business Negotiation

**Characters:** Tom and Rachel are discussing their strategy for an upcoming business negotiation.

**Tom:** "We need to be strategic and not show our hand too early."

**Rachel:** "Agreed. Let's make sure we know the ropes before we start negotiating."

**Tom:** "If we play our cards right, we can come out on top."

**Rachel:** "Yes, but we should be ready to roll with the punches if things don't go as planned."

**Tom:** "Absolutely. Let's aim to beat the clock and finalize the deal quickly."

**Analysis:** In this dialogue, Tom and Rachel use idioms like "show our hand," "know the ropes," "play our cards right," "come out on top," "roll with the punches," and "beat the clock" to discuss their negotiation strategy and contingency plans.

## Dialogue 5: Preparing for a Marathon

**Characters:** Mike and Susan are training for a marathon and discussing their preparation.

**Mike:** "We need to keep our eye on the ball and stick to our training schedule."

**Susan:** "I agree. If we give it our best shot, we'll be ready on race day."

**Mike:** "I'm determined to come out on top this year."

**Susan:** "With your dedication, you might just beat the clock and set a new personal record."

**Mike:** "Thanks, Susan. Let's make sure we're ahead of the game and not leave anything to chance."

**Analysis:** In this dialogue, Mike and Susan use idioms like "keep our eye on the ball," "give it our best shot," "come out on top," "beat the clock," and "ahead of the game" to discuss their marathon preparation and goals.

## Dialogue 6: Academic Project

**Characters:** John and Emily are working on a group project for their college course.

**John:** "We need to brainstorm ideas and get our game plan together."

**Emily:** "Let's make sure we play our cards right to impress the professor."

**John:** "If we hit the books and stay focused, we can come out on top."

**Emily:** "Agreed. We should also roll with the punches if any issues come up."

**John:** "Good point. We can't afford to drop the ball on this project."

**Analysis:** In this dialogue, John and Emily use idioms like "brainstorm," "game plan," "play our cards right," "hit the books," "come out on top," "roll with the punches," and "drop the ball" to discuss their project strategy and preparation.

## Trivia Questions

1. Which idiom means "to make an extra effort beyond what is expected"?
   a) Drop the Ball
   b) Go for the Gold
   c) Go the Extra Mile
   d) Throw in the Towel

2. What does the idiom "hit a home run" signify?

a) To fail

b) To achieve great success

c) To give up

d) To play fairly

3. If someone "throws in the towel," what are they doing?

a) Trying their hardest

b) Admitting defeat

c) Winning easily

d) Making a mistake

4. What does it mean to "take a rain check"?

a) To check the weather forecast

b) To accept an offer

c) To decline an offer but suggest doing it later

d) To fail to complete a task

5. Which idiom describes someone making strategic decisions to maximize their chances of success?

a) Play Hardball

b) Level Playing Field

c) Play Your Cards Right

d) Ahead of the Game

6. What does "come out on top" mean?

a) To win or be the best

b) To fail

c) To give up

d) To try one's hardest

7. If someone is "in the running," what does it mean?
   a) They have no chance of winning
   b) They are a contender
   c) They have already won
   d) They have given up

8. What does it mean to "roll with the punches"?
   a) To fight back aggressively
   b) To adapt to difficult circumstances
   c) To give up easily
   d) To stay focused on the goal

9. Which idiom means "to reveal one's intentions or plans"?
   a) Show One's Hand
   b) Take a Rain Check
   c) Play Hardball
   d) Drop the Ball

10. What does "two strikes against" mean?
   a) Being in a difficult situation
   b) Having an easy time
   c) Winning easily
   d) Making a mistake

## Fun Facts

**Fun Fact #1: Win Hands Down** The phrase "win hands down" originated from horse racing. When a jockey was far enough ahead of the competition, they could drop their hands and relax their grip on the reins, indicating an easy victory.

**Fun Fact #2: Throw in the Towel** This idiom comes from the sport of boxing. When a boxer's corner throws a towel into the ring, it signals that the fighter cannot continue, thereby conceding defeat.

**Fun Fact #3: Hit a Home Run** In baseball, hitting a home run is a notable achievement because it means the batter has successfully hit the ball out of the park, allowing them to run around all the bases and score. This idiom has come to symbolize any significant success.

**Fun Fact #4: Keep Your Eye on the Ball** This idiom comes from sports like baseball and tennis, where players must focus on the ball to perform well. It emphasizes the importance of concentration and focus in achieving success.

**Fun Fact #5: Go for the Gold** This idiom is derived from the Olympics, where athletes strive to win the gold medal, representing the highest achievement in their sport. It encourages aiming for the best possible outcome.

**Fun Fact #6: Come Out on Top** The phrase "come out on top" originally referred to overcoming difficulties and emerging victorious. It's a versatile idiom used in various competitive contexts, emphasizing triumph over challenges.

**Fun Fact #7: Beat the Clock** "Beat the clock" has roots in sporting events where participants must finish tasks within a set time limit. It's now widely used to describe completing any activity before a deadline.

**Fun Fact #8: In the Running** This idiom comes from horse racing, where horses competing for a win are said to be "in the running." It has since been adapted to describe anyone with a chance of winning or succeeding.

**Fun Fact #9: Roll with the Punches** Derived from boxing, "roll with the punches" originally described a technique to avoid the full impact of an opponent's blows. It's now used to describe adapting to and handling difficult situations.

**Fun Fact #10: Show One's Hand** This idiom comes from card games like poker, where players reveal their cards to determine the winner. In everyday use, it emphasizes revealing one's plans or intentions, often strategically.

Learning idioms related to fun and play not only enriches your vocabulary but also makes your language more colorful and expressive. These idioms capture the essence of competition, strategy, and enjoyment associated with sports and games. By practicing these idioms in real-life conversations, quizzes, and games, you can become more comfortable using them and enhance your communication skills. Embrace the playful spirit of these idioms and enjoy the dynamic and engaging ways they can enhance your language.

## Answers

Answer: c) Go the Extra Mile

Answer: b) To achieve great success

Answer: b) Admitting defeat

Answer: c) To decline an offer but suggest doing it later

Answer: c) Play Your Cards Right

Answer: a) To win or be the best

Answer: b) They are a contender

Answer: b) To adapt to difficult circumstances

Answer: a) Show One's Hand

Answer: a) Being in a difficult situation

Chapter 6

# Specialized Idioms

Idioms rooted in history offer a fascinating glimpse into the past, revealing how language evolves with significant events and figures. These idioms often carry rich stories and cultural nuances that make them especially interesting to explore. In this chapter, we delve into specialized idioms that have historical origins. This chapter is divided into sections on idioms derived from historical events, famous figures, and the background stories behind these expressions. Understanding these idioms will not only enhance your vocabulary but also provide a deeper appreciation of the historical contexts from which they emerged.

## Idioms from History

### Historical Events

Many idioms we use today are directly linked to historical events. These idioms encapsulate the essence of significant moments in history, offering a shorthand way to convey complex ideas and emotions. Here are some idioms that originated from historical events:

**1. Crossing the Rubicon**

- **Meaning:** To make an irreversible decision.
- **Example:** "By quitting his job without a backup plan, he crossed the Rubicon."
- **Origin:** This idiom comes from Julius Caesar's decision to cross the Rubicon River with his army in 49 BCE, an act that was considered an insurrection against the Roman Senate and led to a civil war.

**2. Meet Your Waterloo**

- **Meaning:** To encounter one's ultimate defeat.
- **Example:** "The undefeated champion finally met his Waterloo in the final match."
- **Origin:** This phrase references the Battle of Waterloo in 1815, where Napoleon Bonaparte was decisively defeated, marking the end of his reign.

**3. The Die Is Cast**

- **Meaning:** A final decision has been made, and there is no turning back.
- **Example:** "Once they signed the contract, the die was cast."
- **Origin:** Also attributed to Julius Caesar, this phrase refers to the moment he crossed the Rubicon and declared "Alea iacta est" ("The die is cast"), signaling the point of no return.

**4. On the Warpath**

- **Meaning:** Angry and looking for trouble.
- **Example:** "After finding out about the betrayal, she was on the warpath."
- **Origin:** This idiom originates from Native American history, where "going on the warpath" meant preparing for battle.

**5. Worth One's Salt**

- **Meaning:** To be competent and worth one's pay.
- **Example:** "Any employee worth their salt would know how to handle this issue."
- **Origin:** This expression dates back to ancient Rome, where soldiers were often paid in salt, a valuable commodity at the time.

**6. Burn Your Bridges**

- **Meaning:** To destroy one's path, connections, or opportunities, making it impossible to return.
- **Example:** "By insulting his former boss, he burned his bridges."
- **Origin:** This phrase comes from military strategy, where armies would burn bridges after crossing them to prevent retreat or pursuit.

**7. Steal Someone's Thunder**

- **Meaning:** To take credit for someone else's achievements or ideas.

- **Example:** "He stole her thunder by announcing the project as his own."

- **Origin:** This idiom comes from the 18th century, when playwright John Dennis invented a method for creating the sound of thunder for his play. When his play failed, other playwrights used his method, leading Dennis to accuse them of "stealing his thunder."

### 8. Flash in the Pan

- **Meaning:** Something or someone that initially shows promise but fails to deliver.

- **Example:** "His first novel was a bestseller, but he turned out to be a flash in the pan."

- **Origin:** This phrase comes from the early firearms era, where the gunpowder in the pan would ignite but fail to fire the shot, resulting in a disappointing flash.

### 9. Go Over Like a Lead Balloon

- **Meaning:** To fail completely or be poorly received.

- **Example:** "Her suggestion went over like a lead balloon at the meeting."

- **Origin:** This idiom highlights the impossibility of a balloon made of lead floating, metaphorically describing a situation that fails spectacularly.

### 10. Rest on One's Laurels

- **Meaning:** To rely on past achievements and not strive for further success.
- **Example:** "You can't rest on your laurels if you want to stay ahead in this industry."
- **Origin:** This expression dates back to ancient Greece and Rome, where laurels were awarded as a symbol of victory and honor. Resting on one's laurels implies being complacent after previous successes.

**11. Bite the Dust**

- **Meaning:** To fall to the ground, be defeated, or die.
- **Example:** "Many old technologies have bitten the dust in the age of digital innovation."
- **Origin:** This phrase dates back to the 18th century and was popularized by the British army. It likely derives from the imagery of a fallen soldier biting the ground.

**12. Raise the White Flag**

- **Meaning:** To surrender or give up.
- **Example:** "When the team fell behind by 20 points, they essentially raised the white flag."
- **Origin:** The white flag has been a symbol of truce and surrender since at least the Middle Ages.

**13. Pyrrhic Victory**

- **Meaning:** A victory that comes at such a great cost that it is almost tantamount to defeat.
- **Example:** "Winning the lawsuit was a Pyrrhic victory because the legal fees bankrupted the company."
- **Origin:** Named after King Pyrrhus of Epirus, whose army suffered irreplaceable casualties in defeating the Romans at Heraclea in 280 BCE and Asculum in 279 BCE.

### 14. Fiddling While Rome Burns

- **Meaning:** To do something trivial and irresponsible in the midst of an emergency.
- **Example:** "The CEO was accused of fiddling while Rome burned during the company's crisis."
- **Origin:** Refers to the legend that Emperor Nero played the lyre while Rome was consumed by a great fire in 64 CE.

### 15. Shot Heard 'Round the World

- **Meaning:** An event that has international significance.
- **Example:** "The assassination of Archduke Franz Ferdinand was the shot heard 'round the world that led to World War I."
- **Origin:** Originally used to describe the first shot of the American Revolutionary War in 1775.

### 16. Tilting at Windmills

- **Meaning:** Attacking imaginary enemies or fighting unwinnable battles.
- **Example:** "Campaigning against the new policy is like tilting at windmills."
- **Origin:** From Miguel de Cervantes' novel "Don Quixote," where the protagonist mistakes windmills for giants and attempts to fight them.

### 17. Rob Peter to Pay Paul

- **Meaning:** To take from one person or thing to pay another.
- **Example:** "Using credit cards to pay off debt is just robbing Peter to pay Paul."
- **Origin:** This phrase is thought to have originated in the 16th century, potentially relating to the churches of St. Peter and St. Paul in London.

### 18. Cross to Bear

- **Meaning:** A burden or difficult responsibility one must endure.
- **Example:** "Caring for her aging parents is her cross to bear."
- **Origin:** This phrase is derived from the Bible, where Jesus was forced to carry his own cross to his crucifixion.

### 19. Beyond the Pale

- **Meaning:** Outside the bounds of acceptable behavior.

- **Example:** "His actions during the meeting were beyond the pale."
- **Origin:** Refers to the English Pale in Ireland, a region where English rule and law were in effect. Outside this area, behavior was considered unacceptable.

**20. Break the Bank**

- **Meaning:** To use up all of one's resources.
- **Example:** "The unexpected medical bills broke the bank."
- **Origin:** This idiom comes from gambling, where a player winning more money than the casino can pay out is said to "break the bank."

## Famous Figures

Idioms inspired by famous historical figures often reflect their notable actions, characteristics, or events associated with their lives. Here are some idioms derived from well-known individuals:

**1. Achilles' Heel**

- **Meaning:** A person's point of greatest vulnerability.
- **Example:** "His inability to delegate is his Achilles' heel."
- **Origin:** This idiom comes from Greek mythology, where the hero Achilles was invulnerable except for his heel, leading to his downfall when struck there.

**2. Einstein**

- **Meaning:** A person of exceptional intelligence.
- **Example:** "She's the Einstein of our class, always acing every exam."
- **Origin:** This idiom refers to the renowned physicist Albert Einstein, synonymous with genius.

**3. Benedict Arnold**

- **Meaning:** A traitor.
- **Example:** "He was branded a Benedict Arnold after leaking company secrets to a competitor."
- **Origin:** This idiom refers to Benedict Arnold, an American Revolutionary War general who defected to the British side, becoming synonymous with treachery.

**4. Casanova**

- **Meaning:** A man known for having numerous romantic conquests.
- **Example:** "He has a reputation as a real Casanova."
- **Origin:** This idiom comes from Giacomo Casanova, an 18th-century Italian adventurer and writer famous for his romantic escapades.

**5. Draconian**

- **Meaning:** Excessively harsh and severe.
- **Example:** "The new regulations are considered draconian by many employees."

- **Origin:** This idiom refers to Draco, an ancient Athenian lawmaker known for his severe code of laws.

**6. Scrooge**

- **Meaning:** A miserly person.
- **Example:** "Don't be such a Scrooge; it's the season of giving!"
- **Origin:** This idiom comes from Ebenezer Scrooge, the main character in Charles Dickens' "A Christmas Carol," known for his stinginess.

**7. Good Samaritan**

- **Meaning:** A person who helps others in need out of compassion.
- **Example:** "A Good Samaritan stopped to help me change my flat tire."
- **Origin:** This idiom is derived from the Biblical parable of the Good Samaritan, who helped a stranger in need.

**8. Svengali**

- **Meaning:** A person who exercises excessive control or influence over someone.
- **Example:** "The young star was manipulated by her Svengali-like manager."
- **Origin:** This idiom comes from the character Svengali in George du Maurier's novel "Trilby," who controls the titular character through

hypnosis.

### 9. Herculean Task

- **Meaning:** A task requiring great strength or effort.
- **Example:** "Cleaning up after the festival was a Herculean task."
- **Origin:** This idiom refers to Hercules, a hero in Greek mythology known for completing twelve immense and difficult labors.

### 10. Spartan

- **Meaning:** Simple, austere, and disciplined.
- **Example:** "Their lifestyle was spartan, with minimal comforts."
- **Origin:** This idiom comes from the Spartans of ancient Greece, who were known for their austere and disciplined way of life.

### 11. Napoleon Complex

- **Meaning:** A derogatory term for an aggressive or domineering attitude displayed by a short person.
- **Example:** "He's always bossing people around; I think he has a Napoleon complex."
- **Origin:** Named after Napoleon Bonaparte, who was reputed to compensate for his short stature with aggressive behavior.

### 12. Job's Comforter

- **Meaning:** Someone who tries to console another but actually makes them feel worse.

- **Example:** "When he said, 'It could be worse,' it felt like he was being a Job's comforter."
- **Origin:** Refers to the Biblical figure Job, whose friends offered him poor consolation during his suffering.

**13. Darwinian**

- **Meaning:** Relating to the theory of evolution by natural selection or ruthless competition.
- **Example:** "The business world can be quite Darwinian."
- **Origin:** Named after Charles Darwin, who proposed the theory of evolution by natural selection.

**14. Peter Principle**

- **Meaning:** The concept that people in a hierarchy tend to rise to their "level of incompetence."
- **Example:** "His promotion to manager has revealed the Peter Principle in action."
- **Origin:** From the book "The Peter Principle" by Laurence J. Peter, describing how employees are promoted based on their performance in their current role, not their suitability for the new role.

**15. Machiavellian**

- **Meaning:** Cunning, scheming, and unscrupulous, especially in politics.
- **Example:** "His Machiavellian tactics helped him rise to power."
- **Origin:** Named after Niccolò Machiavelli, whose book "The Prince" is seen as a guide for political deceit and manipulation.

**16. Peeping Tom**

- **Meaning:** A person who spies on others, especially in private situations.
- **Example:** "The neighborhood had a Peeping Tom peeking into windows."
- **Origin:** Refers to the legend of Lady Godiva, who rode naked through the streets to gain a remission of the oppressive taxation imposed by her husband. Only one man, Tom, disobeyed her decree to stay indoors and peeped at her.

**17. Uncle Tom**

- **Meaning:** A black person who is overly subservient to white people.
- **Example:** "Some accused him of being an Uncle Tom for siding with the management."
- **Origin:** From Harriet Beecher Stowe's novel "Uncle Tom's Cabin," where the character Uncle Tom is seen as overly submissive.

**18. Catch-22**

- **Meaning:** A paradoxical situation from which there is no escape because of contradictory rules or limitations.
- **Example:** "Needing experience to get a job, but needing a job to get experience is a classic Catch-22."
- **Origin:** From Joseph Heller's novel "Catch-22," where pilots must be declared insane to avoid combat missions, but requesting an evaluation proves their sanity.

**19. Cassandra**

- **Meaning:** A person who prophesies doom or disaster, often ignored.
- **Example:** "She was a Cassandra, warning about the impending crisis that no one believed."
- **Origin:** From Greek mythology, Cassandra was given the gift of prophecy by Apollo, but cursed to never be believed.

**20. Gordian Knot**

- **Meaning:** An extremely complex or difficult problem.
- **Example:** "The company's financial troubles were a Gordian knot that needed untangling."
- **Origin:** From the legend of Gordius, who tied an intricate knot that only Alexander the Great could untangle by cutting through it with his sword.

## Background Stories

The origins of idioms often provide intriguing insights into historical and cultural contexts. Here are some idioms with interesting background stories:

**1. Bite the Bullet**

- **Meaning:** To endure a painful or unpleasant situation with courage.
- **Example:** "You'll just have to bite the bullet and finish the job."
- **Origin:** In the days before anesthesia, soldiers would bite on a bullet during surgery to cope with the pain.

**2. Butter Someone Up**

- **Meaning:** To flatter someone to gain favor.
- **Example:** "He's always buttering up the boss to get a promotion."
- **Origin:** This idiom likely originates from an ancient Indian custom of throwing butter balls at statues of gods to seek favor.

**3. Caught Red-Handed**

- **Meaning:** To be caught in the act of doing something wrong.
- **Example:** "The thief was caught red-handed with the stolen goods."
- **Origin:** This phrase dates back to the 15th century, referring to having blood on one's hands after committing a crime.

**4. Cold Shoulder**

- **Meaning:** To deliberately ignore or show indifference.
- **Example:** "After their argument, she gave him the cold shoulder."
- **Origin:** This idiom comes from the medieval practice of serving a cold shoulder of meat to an unwelcome guest as a subtle hint to leave.

**5. Let the Cat Out of the Bag**

- **Meaning:** To reveal a secret, often unintentionally.
- **Example:** "She let the cat out of the bag about the surprise party."
- **Origin:** This phrase comes from market days when merchants would replace valuable piglets with less valuable cats in a bag. When the buyer discovered the deception, the secret was out.

**6. Pulling Someone's Leg**

- **Meaning:** To tease or joke with someone.
- **Example:** "I was just pulling your leg about winning the lottery."
- **Origin:** The exact origin is unclear, but it may come from 18th-century street thieves who tripped their victims to rob them, making the act of leg-pulling synonymous with fooling someone.

**7. Raining Cats and Dogs**

- **Meaning:** Raining very heavily.
- **Example:** "It's raining cats and dogs outside; don't forget your umbrella."

- **Origin:** This idiom may come from 17th-century England when heavy rains would wash away street debris, including dead animals.

**8. Close But No Cigar**

- **Meaning:** Coming close to success but falling short.
- **Example:** "He almost won the race, but close, but no cigar."
- **Origin:** This phrase originates from carnival games in the early 20th century where cigars were given as prizes. If a player nearly won but didn't succeed, they were "close, but no cigar."

**9. Turn a Blind Eye**

- **Meaning:** To deliberately ignore something.
- **Example:** "The manager turned a blind eye to the employee's tardiness."
- **Origin:** This idiom is attributed to Admiral Horatio Nelson, who supposedly ignored a signal to retreat during a naval battle by holding a telescope to his blind eye.

**10. Break the Ice**

- **Meaning:** To initiate conversation in a social setting, making people feel more comfortable.
- **Example:** "She told a funny story to break the ice at the beginning of the meeting."
- **Origin:** This idiom comes from the practice of breaking ice in

frozen rivers to allow ships to pass through. Just as breaking the ice made it possible for ships to navigate, breaking the ice in a conversation makes it easier for people to connect.

### 11. Cost an Arm and a Leg

- **Meaning:** To be very expensive.
- **Example:** "That designer handbag cost an arm and a leg."
- **Origin:** The exact origin is unclear, but one theory suggests it comes from the high cost of portrait paintings in the 18th century, where full-body portraits were more expensive than those showing just the head and shoulders.

### 12. Under the Weather

- **Meaning:** Feeling ill.
- **Example:** "I'm feeling a bit under the weather today."
- **Origin:** This idiom likely comes from sailors who were sent below deck during bad weather to prevent seasickness, thus being "under the weather."

### 13. Face the Music

- **Meaning:** To confront the consequences of one's actions.
- **Example:** "He had to face the music after getting caught cheating on the exam."
- **Origin:** This idiom may originate from the military, where

disgraced officers were drummed out of their regiment, or from theater, where actors must face the orchestra pit.

### 14. Kick the Bucket

- **Meaning:** To die.
- **Example:** "He kicked the bucket after a long illness."
- **Origin:** This phrase might come from a method of suicide where a person stands on a bucket, ties a noose around their neck, and kicks the bucket away, leading to hanging.

### 15. Wild Goose Chase

- **Meaning:** A futile or hopeless pursuit.
- **Example:** "Searching for her lost keys in the park was a wild goose chase."
- **Origin:** This idiom comes from an old form of horseback racing in which horses followed a lead rider in a manner similar to wild geese following a leader in flight.

### 16. Barking Up the Wrong Tree

- **Meaning:** To pursue a mistaken or misguided course of action.
- **Example:** "If you think I'm the one who took your book, you're barking up the wrong tree."
- **Origin:** This phrase comes from hunting dogs that barked at the base of a tree where they mistakenly thought their prey was hiding.

### 17. Throw Down the Gauntlet

- **Meaning:** To challenge someone.
- **Example:** "He threw down the gauntlet by daring his rival to a duel."
- **Origin:** In medieval times, knights would throw down a gauntlet (a type of glove) as a challenge to combat. Picking it up signified acceptance of the challenge.

### 18. By the Skin of Your Teeth

- **Meaning:** Barely succeeding in doing something.
- **Example:** "He passed the exam by the skin of his teeth."
- **Origin:** This phrase comes from the Bible, specifically the Book of Job, where Job says, "I am escaped with the skin of my teeth," implying a narrow escape.

### 19. Cold Feet

- **Meaning:** To feel nervous or unsure about something.
- **Example:** "She got cold feet just before her wedding."
- **Origin:** The origin is uncertain, but it may come from soldiers who were unable to fight because of frozen feet, thus being unable to proceed.

### 20. Mad as a Hatter

- **Meaning:** Completely insane.

- **Example:** "He's mad as a hatter if he thinks he can climb that mountain without any training."
- **Origin:** This idiom comes from the hat-making industry in the 18th and 19th centuries, where mercury used in the production process caused hatters to suffer from mercury poisoning, leading to erratic behavior.

Exploring idioms from history not only enhances your understanding of language but also provides fascinating insights into the cultural and historical contexts from which these expressions emerged. By delving into idioms derived from historical events, famous figures, and interesting background stories, you gain a richer appreciation of how language evolves and captures the essence of significant moments in time. As you incorporate these idioms into your vocabulary, you'll find your communication more colorful, expressive, and enriched with historical depth.

# Chapter 7
# Regional Idioms

Regional idioms capture the unique cultural and geographical influences of different areas, reflecting the local history, traditions, and ways of life. In this chapter, we delve into idioms from the western regions of the United States, including the Pacific Coast and the Mountain Region. These idioms offer a glimpse into the distinct character of these areas, enhancing your language with regional flair and authenticity.

## Idioms from the West

The Western United States, known for its diverse landscapes and rich cultural heritage, has produced a variety of idioms that reflect its unique character. From the bustling cities along the Pacific Coast to the rugged terrain of the Mountain Region, these idioms are imbued with the spirit and history of the West.

## Pacific Coast Sayings

The Pacific Coast, stretching from California to Washington, is renowned for its coastal beauty, vibrant cities, and laid-back lifestyle. The idioms from this region often reflect the relaxed, innovative, and nature-loving ethos of the West Coast.

**1. Catch the Wave**

- **Meaning:** To take advantage of a trend or opportunity.
- **Example:** "The tech company caught the wave of the internet boom and quickly became a market leader."
- **Usage:** This idiom is inspired by surfing, a popular activity along the Pacific Coast, and suggests seizing opportunities as they arise.

**2. Go with the Flow**

- **Meaning:** To be relaxed and accept things as they come.
- **Example:** "On vacation, we decided to go with the flow and explore without a strict itinerary."
- **Usage:** Reflecting the laid-back attitude of the West Coast, this idiom encourages flexibility and adaptability.

**3. California Dreaming**

- **Meaning:** Having optimistic and ambitious dreams, often associated with the lifestyle and opportunities in California.
- **Example:** "She moved to Los Angeles, California dreaming of becoming a Hollywood star."
- **Usage:** This idiom evokes the aspirational and often idyllic vision of life in California.

**4. Hang Ten**

- **Meaning:** To perform skillfully or excel at something, particularly in a casual or nonchalant manner.
- **Example:** "He really hung ten during his presentation, impressing everyone with his knowledge."
- **Usage:** Originating from surfing, where "hanging ten" refers to a maneuver where the surfer's toes hang over the board's edge, this idiom celebrates cool competence.

**5. Laid-Back Attitude**

- **Meaning:** A relaxed, easy-going approach to life.
- **Example:** "Her laid-back attitude makes her a pleasure to work with, even during stressful projects."
- **Usage:** This idiom embodies the West Coast's reputation for a relaxed lifestyle.

**6. Ride the Wave**

- **Meaning:** To take advantage of a current trend or movement.
- **Example:** "The startup rode the wave of renewable energy and found great success."
- **Usage:** Similar to "catch the wave," this idiom highlights the importance of leveraging trends for success.

**7. Coast Along**

- **Meaning:** To proceed or succeed with little effort or resistance.
- **Example:** "With her experience, she can coast along in her new role without any problems."
- **Usage:** This idiom reflects the ease of life and work that is often associated with the Pacific Coast.

**8. In the Groove**

- **Meaning:** Performing well and confidently, often in a consistent manner.
- **Example:** "After a few practice sessions, the band was in the groove and ready to perform."
- **Usage:** Originating from the music scene, this idiom captures the rhythm and flow that characterize successful performance.

**9. Beach Bum**

- **Meaning:** Someone who spends a lot of time relaxing at the beach.
- **Example:** "He turned into a real beach bum after moving to Malibu."
- **Usage:** This idiom playfully describes someone who enjoys the relaxed, sun-soaked lifestyle of the coast.

**10. Surf's Up**

- **Meaning:** A call to action, especially to join in something exciting or enjoyable.

- **Example:** "Surf's up! Let's head to the beach and enjoy the waves."
- **Usage:** Originally a surfer's call, this idiom now broadly signifies a moment of opportunity or excitement.

**11. Catch Some Rays**

- **Meaning:** To sunbathe or spend time in the sun.
- **Example:** "I plan to catch some rays this weekend at the beach."
- **Usage:** Reflecting the sunny climate of the Pacific Coast, this idiom emphasizes relaxation and enjoyment.

**12. Sunny Disposition**

- **Meaning:** A cheerful and optimistic attitude.
- **Example:** "Her sunny disposition makes her popular with colleagues and friends alike."
- **Usage:** Inspired by the region's sunny weather, this idiom describes a positive and upbeat personality.

**13. Coastal Chill**

- **Meaning:** A relaxed and carefree attitude.
- **Example:** "After moving to Santa Cruz, he adopted a coastal chill lifestyle."
- **Usage:** This idiom captures the easy-going nature of coastal living.

**14. Tinseltown**

- **Meaning:** A nickname for Hollywood, referring to its glamorous and superficial aspects.
- **Example:** "She moved to Tinseltown to pursue her acting dreams."
- **Usage:** This idiom reflects the allure and sometimes illusory nature of Hollywood fame.

**15. Go Off the Deep End**

- **Meaning:** To act recklessly or irrationally.
- **Example:** "When he heard the news, he went off the deep end and made some hasty decisions."
- **Usage:** Borrowed from swimming, this idiom warns against impulsive actions.

**16. Dive Right In**

- **Meaning:** To begin something enthusiastically and without hesitation.
- **Example:** "She decided to dive right in and start her own business."
- **Usage:** Reflecting the adventurous spirit of the coast, this idiom encourages bold action.

**17. Pacific Paradise**

- **Meaning:** A term describing the idyllic beauty and tranquility of coastal areas.
- **Example:** "They spent their honeymoon in a Pacific paradise,

enjoying the serene beaches."

- **Usage:** This idiom celebrates the natural beauty and appeal of the Pacific Coast.

**18. West Coast Cool**

- **Meaning:** A stylish and relaxed approach to life and fashion.
- **Example:** "Her West Coast cool style always turns heads at parties."
- **Usage:** This idiom highlights the unique blend of casual elegance found in the region.

**19. Flip-Flop Mentality**

- **Meaning:** A casual and flexible approach to decision-making and life.
- **Example:** "Adopting a flip-flop mentality helped him adapt to the ever-changing tech industry."
- **Usage:** Reflecting the laid-back nature of the coast, this idiom encourages adaptability and openness.

**20. Go Coastal**

- **Meaning:** To embrace a relaxed and carefree lifestyle.
- **Example:** "After years in the corporate world, he decided to go coastal and move to a beach town."
- **Usage:** This idiom captures the transition to a more relaxed and enjoyable way of living.

## Mountain Region Phrases

The Mountain Region, encompassing states like Colorado, Wyoming, Montana, and Idaho, is characterized by its rugged landscapes, outdoor activities, and pioneering spirit. Idioms from this area often reflect the toughness, self-reliance, and adventurous nature of life in the mountains.

### 1. Mountain to Climb

- **Meaning:** A significant challenge or obstacle to overcome.
- **Example:** "Starting his own business was a mountain to climb, but he persevered."
- **Usage:** This idiom emphasizes the difficulty and effort required to achieve a goal.

### 2. On Top of the World

- **Meaning:** Feeling extremely happy and successful.
- **Example:** "After winning the competition, she felt on top of the world."
- **Usage:** Reflecting the majestic peaks of the region, this idiom conveys a sense of triumph and elation.

### 3. Rough and Ready

- **Meaning:** Crude but effective and prepared for action.
- **Example:** "The cabin was rough and ready, but it served its purpose well."

- **Usage:** This idiom highlights the practical and resilient nature of mountain life.

**4. Off the Beaten Path**

- **Meaning:** In an isolated or less known area.
- **Example:** "They found a beautiful campsite off the beaten path."
- **Usage:** Reflecting the remote and untouched landscapes of the mountains, this idiom encourages exploration beyond the usual routes.

**5. High as a Kite**

- **Meaning:** Extremely happy or excited; also, intoxicated.
- **Example:** "He was high as a kite after getting his dream job."
- **Usage:** This idiom uses the image of soaring high to convey intense emotions or states.

**6. Over the Hill**

- **Meaning:** Past one's prime or considered too old.
- **Example:** "Some people think he's over the hill, but he continues to outperform younger colleagues."
- **Usage:** This idiom reflects the natural imagery of mountains and hills to describe aging.

**7. Rocky Road**

- **Meaning:** A difficult or challenging path.
- **Example:** "The startup faced a rocky road in its first year, but things eventually stabilized."
- **Usage:** Inspired by the rugged terrain of the mountains, this idiom emphasizes challenges and obstacles.

**8. Climb the Mountain**

- **Meaning:** To undertake a significant and often difficult task.
- **Example:** "He decided to climb the mountain and write a book about his experiences."
- **Usage:** This idiom symbolizes the effort and determination required to achieve lofty goals.

**9. Hit the Trail**

- **Meaning:** To begin a journey or start traveling.
- **Example:** "They packed their gear and hit the trail early in the morning."
- **Usage:** Reflecting the outdoor lifestyle of the mountain region, this idiom encourages adventure and movement.

**10. Pinnacle of Success**

- **Meaning:** The highest point of achievement or success.
- **Example:** "Winning the award was the pinnacle of his career."

- **Usage:** Using the imagery of mountain peaks, this idiom celebrates reaching the top.

### 11. Snowball Effect

- **Meaning:** A situation where something increases in size or significance at an accelerating rate.
- **Example:** "The company's growth had a snowball effect, rapidly expanding its market presence."
- **Usage:** Inspired by the natural phenomenon of snowballs growing larger as they roll, this idiom describes exponential growth or consequences.

### 12. Avalanche of Problems

- **Meaning:** A sudden, overwhelming flood of difficulties.
- **Example:** "After the initial mistake, an avalanche of problems followed."
- **Usage:** Reflecting the powerful and often destructive nature of avalanches, this idiom conveys a sense of overwhelming challenges.

### 13. Scale the Heights

- **Meaning:** To achieve great success or reach a high level.
- **Example:** "She scaled the heights of her profession, becoming a top executive."
- **Usage:** This idiom uses the imagery of climbing to great heights to

symbolize achieving success.

**14. Bear the Brunt**

- **Meaning:** To endure the worst part of something.
- **Example:** "During the storm, the coastal areas bore the brunt of the damage."
- **Usage:** Reflecting the harsh conditions often faced in the mountains, this idiom emphasizes enduring hardship.

**15. At the Summit**

- **Meaning:** At the highest point of achievement or success.
- **Example:** "He felt he was at the summit of his career after receiving the industry award."
- **Usage:** Using the imagery of mountain summits, this idiom celebrates reaching the highest levels of success.

**16. Clear the Hurdles**

- **Meaning:** To overcome obstacles or difficulties.
- **Example:** "Despite many setbacks, she managed to clear the hurdles and complete her degree."
- **Usage:** This idiom highlights the effort required to overcome challenges, using the imagery of clearing physical barriers.

**17. Cold Shoulder**

- **Meaning:** To intentionally ignore or reject someone.
- **Example:** "After their argument, he gave her the cold shoulder."
- **Usage:** Reflecting the chilly climate of the mountains, this idiom describes social rejection.

**18. Trailblazer**

- **Meaning:** A person who is the first to do something or who opens the way for others.
- **Example:** "As a woman in tech, she was a trailblazer in her field."
- **Usage:** This idiom celebrates pioneers and innovators, using the imagery of creating new paths.

**19. Rough Terrain**

- **Meaning:** Difficult or challenging circumstances.
- **Example:** "The project encountered some rough terrain, but they persevered."
- **Usage:** Inspired by the rugged landscapes of the mountain region, this idiom emphasizes challenges.

**20. Take the High Road**

- **Meaning:** To act with integrity and honor, especially in difficult situations.
- **Example:** "Even when criticized, she always takes the high road and responds with grace."

- **Usage:** This idiom uses the imagery of choosing a higher, more difficult path to symbolize moral integrity.

## Cultural Influences

Regional idioms are often shaped by the cultural influences unique to their areas. The Pacific Coast and Mountain Region are no exceptions, each drawing from their distinct historical, social, and environmental contexts to create idioms that resonate with the local populations.

## Pacific Coast Cultural Influences

The Pacific Coast, with its rich history of exploration, innovation, and environmental consciousness, has idioms that reflect these themes. The cultural melting pot of California, the tech hubs of Silicon Valley and Seattle, and the eco-friendly attitudes prevalent in the region all contribute to the creation of idioms that embody these values.

### 1. Silicon Valley Mindset

- **Meaning:** An innovative and entrepreneurial attitude.
- **Example:** "She brought a Silicon Valley mindset to the startup, driving rapid growth."
- **Usage:** This idiom reflects the innovative spirit of the tech industry centered in California's Silicon Valley.

### 2. Green Living

- **Meaning:** A lifestyle focused on environmental sustainability.

- **Example:** "The community promotes green living through recycling programs and renewable energy."
- **Usage:** Reflecting the eco-conscious culture of the West Coast, this idiom emphasizes sustainable practices.

3. **La-La Land**

- **Meaning:** A fanciful or unrealistic state of mind.
- **Example:** "If you think you can finish this project in one day, you're living in La-La Land."
- **Usage:** Originating as a nickname for Los Angeles, this idiom describes unrealistic expectations or daydreaming.

4. **Tech Savvy**

- **Meaning:** Highly skilled with technology.
- **Example:** "The new generation is incredibly tech savvy, adapting quickly to new gadgets."
- **Usage:** Reflecting the high-tech culture of the Pacific Coast, this idiom celebrates technological proficiency.

5. **Eco-Warrior**

- **Meaning:** A person actively involved in environmental protection.
- **Example:** "As an eco-warrior, she leads initiatives to reduce plastic waste."
- **Usage:** This idiom highlights the activism and environmental

consciousness prevalent in the region.

**6. Hollywood Ending**

- **Meaning:** A happy and satisfying conclusion, often unrealistic.
- **Example:** "The negotiations ended with a Hollywood ending, pleasing all parties."
- **Usage:** Reflecting the influence of the film industry, this idiom describes idealistic resolutions.

**7. Tech Boom**

- **Meaning:** A period of rapid growth in the technology sector.
- **Example:** "The city experienced a tech boom, attracting numerous startups and investors."
- **Usage:** This idiom captures the explosive growth and opportunities in the tech industry.

**8. Wine Country**

- **Meaning:** A region known for its wine production and vineyards.
- **Example:** "They spent the weekend touring wine country and sampling local vintages."
- **Usage:** Reflecting the famous wine-producing regions of California, this idiom emphasizes quality and indulgence.

**9. Zen Out**

- **Meaning:** To relax and achieve a state of calm.
- **Example:** "After a stressful day, she likes to zen out with some yoga."
- **Usage:** Inspired by the mindfulness and wellness culture of the West Coast, this idiom promotes relaxation.

**10. Sunshine State of Mind**

- **Meaning:** A positive and optimistic attitude.
- **Example:** "With her sunshine state of mind, she always sees the bright side of things."
- **Usage:** Reflecting the sunny disposition associated with the Pacific Coast, this idiom emphasizes positivity.

## Mountain Region Cultural Influences

The Mountain Region's idioms are shaped by its history of exploration, mining, ranching, and outdoor adventure. The self-reliance and resilience required to thrive in this rugged environment are reflected in the idioms that have emerged from this area.

**1. Gold Rush Spirit**

- **Meaning:** The adventurous and opportunistic attitude of seeking fortune.
- **Example:** "He approached his new business venture with a gold rush spirit."
- **Usage:** Reflecting the historical Gold Rush, this idiom celebrates

ambition and risk-taking.

**2. Pioneer Spirit**

- **Meaning:** The willingness to take risks and venture into unknown territories.
- **Example:** "Her pioneer spirit drove her to explore new business opportunities."
- **Usage:** This idiom honors the adventurous and resilient attitude of early settlers.

**3. Saddle Up**

- **Meaning:** To prepare for action or embark on a task.
- **Example:** "It's time to saddle up and start the project."
- **Usage:** Reflecting the region's ranching heritage, this idiom emphasizes readiness and action.

**4. Frontier Justice**

- **Meaning:** Rough and immediate justice, often outside formal legal systems.
- **Example:** "The town dealt with the outlaws through frontier justice."
- **Usage:** This idiom captures the rough-and-ready approach to justice in the untamed West.

**5. Mountain Man**

- **Meaning:** A person who is rugged and self-sufficient, living in remote areas.
- **Example:** "He lived like a mountain man, far from the conveniences of modern life."
- **Usage:** Reflecting the solitary and hardy lifestyle of early trappers and explorers, this idiom celebrates self-sufficiency.

**6. Trail Mix**

- **Meaning:** A mixture of elements or factors.
- **Example:** "The committee was a trail mix of experts from different fields."
- **Usage:** Inspired by the practical snack for hikers, this idiom emphasizes diversity and variety.

**7. Mining for Gold**

- **Meaning:** Searching for valuable opportunities or information.
- **Example:** "They were mining for gold in the data to find market insights."
- **Usage:** Reflecting the region's mining history, this idiom celebrates the search for value.

**8. Rocky Mountain High**

- **Meaning:** A state of euphoria or happiness, often from nature or physical activity.

- **Example:** "After reaching the summit, he experienced a Rocky Mountain high."
- **Usage:** This idiom captures the exhilaration of outdoor adventures in the mountains.

**9. Rugged Individualism**

- **Meaning:** The belief in self-reliance and independence.
- **Example:** "Her rugged individualism drove her to start her own business."
- **Usage:** Reflecting the frontier spirit, this idiom celebrates independence and self-sufficiency.

**10. Out in the Sticks**

- **Meaning:** In a remote or rural area.
- **Example:** "They built their cabin out in the sticks, far from the city."
- **Usage:** This idiom emphasizes isolation and the rural nature of many mountain communities.

Exploring regional idioms from the Pacific Coast and Mountain Region not only enhances your understanding of language but also provides fascinating insights into the cultural and geographical contexts from which these expressions emerged. These idioms capture the essence of their regions, offering a rich tapestry of history, culture, and lifestyle. By incorporating these idioms into your vocabulary, you'll find your communication more colorful, expressive, and enriched with regional authenticity. As you embrace these idioms, you celebrate the diversity and uniqueness of the American linguistic landscape.

## Chapter 8

# Practice and Application

Mastering idioms is a crucial part of becoming proficient in any language. Idioms add color and nuance to our expressions, making our communication more engaging and effective. In this chapter, we will focus on the practical application of idioms, particularly in writing. Whether you're crafting an essay, engaging in creative writing, or providing peer feedback, understanding how to use idioms effectively can greatly enhance your writing skills.

### Using Idioms in Writing

Idioms can significantly enrich your writing by adding depth and personality. However, using idioms effectively requires a nuanced understanding of their meanings and connotations. Here are some key considerations for using idioms in your writing:

### Context is Key

The context in which an idiom is used is crucial to its effectiveness. Using an idiom inappropriately can confuse your readers or detract from your message. For example, the idiom "hit the sack" means to go to bed, so it would be out of place in a formal business report but perfect for a casual narrative.

**Example:**

- Appropriate: "After a long day of hiking, I was ready to hit the sack."
- Inappropriate: "The company's quarterly report was so comprehensive that I needed to hit the sack immediately."

## Understand the Idiom's Meaning

Before using an idiom, ensure you fully understand its meaning and connotations. Misusing idioms can lead to misunderstandings or make your writing seem less credible.

**Example:**

- Correct: "He was a tough nut to crack, but eventually, we got him to open up."
- Incorrect: "He was a tough nut to crack, but eventually, we managed to break him."

## Match the Tone

Idioms can be informal, formal, humorous, or serious. Choose idioms that match the tone of your writing. Using an informal idiom in a formal context can undermine the professionalism of your work.

**Example:**

- Formal: "The situation was dire, and the company's prospects were hanging by a thread."

- Informal: "The situation was dire, and the company's prospects were hanging on by the skin of their teeth."

### Avoid Overuse

While idioms can enhance your writing, overusing them can make your writing seem forced or contrived. Use idioms sparingly and ensure they add value to your narrative.

**Example:**

- Balanced: "She had a heart of gold, always willing to lend a hand when needed."
- Overuse: "She had a heart of gold, and whenever someone was in a pickle, she would bend over backward to help, even if it meant burning the midnight oil."

## Incorporating Idioms in Essays

Essays, whether academic or personal, can benefit from the judicious use of idioms. They can add flair and emphasis, making your arguments more persuasive and your narrative more engaging.

### Academic Essays

In academic essays, idioms should be used with caution. While they can make your writing more vivid, they should not replace clear and precise language.

Use idioms to highlight key points or to add a touch of personality to your writing.

**Example:**

- Thesis Statement: "The phenomenon of climate change is a ticking time bomb that demands immediate action."
- Supporting Argument: "If we continue to drag our feet, the repercussions will be irreversible."

## Personal Essays

Personal essays are more flexible and allow for a more liberal use of idioms. They can help convey your voice and make your narrative more relatable and engaging.

**Example:**

- Introduction: "Growing up in a small town, I learned that the grass isn't always greener on the other side."
- Conclusion: "In the end, I realized that home is where the heart is, and no amount of wandering could change that."

## Structuring Your Essay with Idioms

Use idioms to create a memorable introduction, emphasize key points in the body, and craft a compelling conclusion. Ensure that the idioms you choose enhance your message and fit naturally into your writing.

**Example:**

- Introduction: "As the saying goes, 'a picture is worth a thousand words.' This adage rings especially true in the realm of advertising."
- Body: "First and foremost, capturing the audience's attention is crucial. As marketers often say, 'you never get a second chance to make a first impression.'"
- Conclusion: "In summary, the power of visual storytelling cannot be overstated. Indeed, 'seeing is believing.'"

## Creative Writing with Idioms

Creative writing provides the perfect canvas for idioms. They can add color, humor, and depth to your stories, poems, and plays. Here are some tips for incorporating idioms into your creative writing:

### Character Development

Use idioms to reveal your characters' personalities, backgrounds, and emotions. A character who frequently uses idioms might be seen as folksy or down-to-earth.

**Example:**

- "Jake was a salt-of-the-earth kind of guy. He believed in rolling up his sleeves and getting the job done."

### Setting the Scene

Idioms can help set the scene and create a vivid picture for your readers. They can convey time, place, and atmosphere in a few words.

**Example:**

- "The little town was quiet as a mouse, with only the distant hum of the highway breaking the silence."

## Dialogue

Incorporate idioms into your characters' dialogue to make it more realistic and engaging. This can also help differentiate characters and give them distinct voices.

**Example:**

- "Don't get your knickers in a twist, Sam," she said, laughing. "We'll figure this out."

## Adding Humor

Idioms can be a great source of humor in creative writing. Play with literal interpretations or use unexpected idioms to surprise your readers.

**Example:**

- "He was so clumsy, it was like a bull in a china shop had taken ballet lessons from him."

## Enhancing Descriptions

Use idioms to enhance your descriptions and make them more dynamic. They can convey complex ideas and emotions in a relatable way.

**Example:**

- "Her excitement was palpable, and she was grinning from ear to ear."

## Writing Prompts

Here are some writing prompts to help you practice incorporating idioms into your own sentences. Try to use at least one idiom in each response.

### Prompt 1: A Memorable Trip

Write about a memorable trip you took. Describe the places you visited, the people you met, and the experiences you had, using idioms to bring your narrative to life.

**Example:**

- "During my trip to Italy, I hit the jackpot with a local guide who showed me the hidden gems of Rome. The experience was a dream come true, and I felt on top of the world."

### Prompt 2: Overcoming a Challenge

Write about a time you faced and overcame a significant challenge. Use idioms to describe your emotions and the steps you took to overcome the obstacle.

**Example:**

- "When I started my own business, it felt like I was swimming against the tide. But with determination and hard work, I eventually turned the corner and saw the light at the end of the tunnel."

## Prompt 3: A Surprising Event

Write about a surprising event that happened to you. Use idioms to capture the shock, excitement, or confusion you felt.

**Example:**

- "When I won the lottery, it was like a bolt from the blue. I was over the moon, and for a moment, it felt like I was walking on air."

## Prompt 4: A Lesson Learned

Write about an important lesson you learned in life. Use idioms to illustrate the key points and make your narrative more engaging.

**Example:**

- "I learned the hard way that you can't judge a book by its cover. It was a tough pill to swallow, but it taught me to look beyond appearances."

## Prompt 5: An Unforgettable Experience

Write about an unforgettable experience you've had. Use idioms to describe the sights, sounds, and feelings you encountered.

**Example:**

- "Skydiving for the first time was an unforgettable experience. The adrenaline rush was like riding a roller coaster, and I felt as free as a bird."

Mastering the use of idioms in writing can greatly enhance your communication skills, making your narratives more engaging and expressive. By understanding the context, meaning, and appropriate usage of idioms, you can incorporate them effectively into various types of writing, from essays to creative pieces. Practice using idioms through writing prompts and be open to feedback to continually improve your idiomatic usage. Embrace the richness that idioms bring to language, and let them add color and depth to your writing.

Through this chapter, you now have a comprehensive guide to using idioms in your writing. With practice, feedback, and a keen understanding of idiomatic expressions, you can elevate your writing and communicate with greater flair and nuance. Happy writing!

Chapter 9

# Idioms Reference List

## A

### A Blessing in Disguise

- **Meaning:** Something that seems bad at first but turns out to be good.
- **Example:** "Losing that job was a blessing in disguise; it pushed me to pursue my true passion."

### A Bird in the Hand is Worth Two in the Bush

- **Meaning:** It's better to have a sure thing than to risk it for something more uncertain.
- **Example:** "I know this job isn't perfect, but a bird in the hand is worth two in the bush."

### A Chip on Your Shoulder

- **Meaning:** Being upset for something that happened in the past.

- **Example:** "He has a chip on his shoulder about not getting the promotion."

### A Dime a Dozen

- **Meaning:** Something very common and not particularly valuable.
- **Example:** "Those souvenirs are a dime a dozen at the market."

### A Leopard Can't Change Its Spots

- **Meaning:** One cannot change their inherent nature.
- **Example:** "He'll never be punctual; a leopard can't change its spots."

### A Penny for Your Thoughts

- **Meaning:** Asking someone what they are thinking.
- **Example:** "You've been quiet for a while – a penny for your thoughts?"

### A Piece of Cake

- **Meaning:** Something very easy to do.
- **Example:** "Once you get the hang of it, riding a bike is a piece of cake."

### A Slap on the Wrist

- **Meaning:** A mild punishment.
- **Example:** "He got a slap on the wrist for breaking the rules."

### A Stitch in Time Saves Nine

- **Meaning:** Taking care of problems before they worsen is beneficial.
- **Example:** "Fix the leak now; a stitch in time saves nine."

### A Storm in a Teacup

- **Meaning:** A lot of fuss over something trivial.
- **Example:** "Their argument was just a storm in a teacup."

### A Taste of Your Own Medicine

- **Meaning:** Being treated the same way you have treated others.
- **Example:** "When the prankster got pranked, he finally got a taste of his own medicine."

### A Toss-Up

- **Meaning:** A situation where the outcome is uncertain and could go either way.
- **Example:** "It's a toss-up whether the weather will be good for our picnic."

### Ace in the Hole

- **Meaning:** A hidden advantage or resource kept in reserve until needed.
- **Example:** "Her experience in negotiations is her ace in the hole."

**Achilles' Heel**

- **Meaning:** A weakness or vulnerable point.
- **Example:** "Despite his strong performance, his Achilles' heel is his poor time management."

**Actions Speak Louder Than Words**

- **Meaning:** What someone actually does means more than what they say they will do.
- **Example:** "She promised to help, but actions speak louder than words – I'll believe it when I see it."

**Add Fuel to the Fire**

- **Meaning:** To make a bad situation worse.
- **Example:** "His comments only added fuel to the fire during the heated argument."

**Against the Clock**

- **Meaning:** Rushed and working quickly to meet a deadline.
- **Example:** "We're racing against the clock to finish the project on time."

**All Bark and No Bite**

- **Meaning:** Someone who talks tough but doesn't act on their threats.

- **Example:** "He's all bark and no bite; he won't actually follow through with his threats."

**All in the Same Boat**

- **Meaning:** Everyone in the same situation.
- **Example:** "During the pandemic, we realized we're all in the same boat."

**All That Glitters Is Not Gold**

- **Meaning:** Not everything that looks valuable is actually valuable.
- **Example:** "Be careful with those investment opportunities – all that glitters is not gold."

**At the Drop of a Hat**

- **Meaning:** Immediately, without any hesitation.
- **Example:** "She's ready to travel at the drop of a hat."

## B

### Back to Square One

- **Meaning:** Returning to the beginning due to a failure or setback.
- **Example:** "The project failed, so we're back to square one."

### Back to the Drawing Board

- **Meaning:** Starting over again because the previous attempt failed.
- **Example:** "When the prototype failed, we went back to the drawing board."

### Ballpark Figure

- **Meaning:** An approximate number.
- **Example:** "Can you give me a ballpark figure of the costs?"

### Barking Up the Wrong Tree

- **Meaning:** Pursuing the wrong course of action or blaming the wrong person.
- **Example:** "If you think I took your book, you're barking up the wrong tree."

### Beat Around the Bush

- **Meaning:** To avoid getting to the point.
- **Example:** "Stop beating around the bush and tell me what you

want."

### Beating a Dead Horse

- **Meaning:** Continuing to pursue a lost cause.
- **Example:** "We're just beating a dead horse trying to change his mind."

### Best of Both Worlds

- **Meaning:** Benefiting from two different opportunities or situations.
- **Example:** "Living in the city and working from home gives me the best of both worlds."

### Between a Rock and a Hard Place

- **Meaning:** Facing two difficult choices.
- **Example:** "I was between a rock and a hard place trying to decide between the two job offers."

### Birds of a Feather Flock Together

- **Meaning:** People with similar interests or characteristics tend to associate with each other.
- **Example:** "Those two are always together; birds of a feather flock together."

### Bite Off More Than You Can Chew

- **Meaning:** Taking on more than one can handle.
- **Example:** "I bit off more than I could chew when I agreed to take on those extra projects."

**Bite the Bullet**

- **Meaning:** To endure a painful or unpleasant situation that is unavoidable.
- **Example:** "I hate going to the dentist, but I'll just have to bite the bullet."

**Bite the Dust**

- **Meaning:** To fail or be defeated.
- **Example:** "Many startups bite the dust within the first year."

**Break the Bank**

- **Meaning:** To be very expensive.
- **Example:** "I'd love to buy a new car, but I don't want to break the bank."

**Break the Ice**

- **Meaning:** To initiate conversation in a social setting, making people feel more comfortable.
- **Example:** "She told a funny story to break the ice at the beginning of the meeting."

**Burn the Midnight Oil**

- **Meaning:** To work late into the night.
- **Example:** "I had to burn the midnight oil to finish the project on time."

**Burn Your Bridges**

- **Meaning:** Destroying one's path, connections, or opportunities, making it impossible to return.
- **Example:** "By insulting his former boss, he burned his bridges."

**Bury the Hatchet**

- **Meaning:** To make peace and stop arguing.
- **Example:** "After years of rivalry, the two companies finally buried the hatchet."

**Bury Your Head in the Sand**

- **Meaning:** To ignore or avoid reality or responsibility.
- **Example:** "You can't just bury your head in the sand and hope the problem goes away."

**By the Skin of Your Teeth**

- **Meaning:** Barely succeeding in doing something.
- **Example:** "He passed the exam by the skin of his teeth."

## C

### Call It a Day

- **Meaning:** To stop working for the day.
- **Example:** "We've done enough work today; let's call it a day."

### Can't Judge a Book by Its Cover

- **Meaning:** Not judging someone or something based on appearance.
- **Example:** "She looked unassuming, but you can't judge a book by its cover."

### Caught Between a Rock and a Hard Place

- **Meaning:** Facing two equally difficult choices.
- **Example:** "She's caught between a rock and a hard place, choosing between her job and her family."

### Caught Between Two Stools

- **Meaning:** When someone finds it difficult to choose between two alternatives.
- **Example:** "He was caught between two stools, trying to decide between his career and family."

### Caught Red-Handed

- **Meaning:** To be caught in the act of doing something wrong.

- **Example:** "The thief was caught red-handed with the stolen goods."

**Cry Over Spilled Milk**

- **Meaning:** To be upset about something that cannot be undone.
- **Example:** "It's no use crying over spilled milk; what's done is done."

**Cry Wolf**

- **Meaning:** To raise a false alarm.
- **Example:** "If you keep crying wolf, no one will believe you when you really need help."

**Cut and Dried**

- **Meaning:** Simple and straightforward.
- **Example:** "The rules are cut and dried; there's no room for interpretation."

**Cut Corners**

- **Meaning:** To do something in the easiest or cheapest way.
- **Example:** "They cut corners to save money, which affected the quality of their work."

**Cut to the Chase**

- **Meaning:** To get to the point without wasting time.
- **Example:** "Let's cut to the chase and discuss the main issues."

**Curiosity Killed the Cat**

- **Meaning:** Being too curious can lead to trouble.
- **Example:** "Be careful with that old house; curiosity killed the cat."

## D

### Dark Horse

- **Meaning:** A little-known person or thing that emerges to prominence.
- **Example:** "The candidate was a dark horse, surprising everyone by winning the election."

### Dead Ringer

- **Meaning:** An exact duplicate.
- **Example:** "He's a dead ringer for his father."

### Devil's Advocate

- **Meaning:** Someone who argues a point to provoke discussion.
- **Example:** "I'm not against your idea, but let me play devil's advocate for a moment."

### Don't Count Your Chickens Before They Hatch

- **Meaning:** Don't assume you'll get something before it's certain.
- **Example:** "Don't count your chickens before they hatch; wait until you have the offer in writing."

### Don't Put All Your Eggs in One Basket

- **Meaning:** Don't risk everything on a single venture.

- **Example:** "Diversify your investments; don't put all your eggs in one basket."

**Drastic Times Call for Drastic Measures**

- **Meaning:** Extreme circumstances require extreme actions.
- **Example:** "With the company struggling, the CEO decided that drastic times call for drastic measures."

**Drive Up the Wall**

- **Meaning:** To irritate or annoy someone intensely.
- **Example:** "Her constant complaints drive me up the wall."

## E

### Eager Beaver

- **Meaning:** Someone who is very enthusiastic and hardworking.
- **Example:** "She's an eager beaver who always volunteers for extra work."

### Elephant in the Room

- **Meaning:** An obvious problem or issue that people avoid discussing.
- **Example:** "The company's financial troubles were the elephant in the room during the meeting."

### Elbow Room

- **Meaning:** Enough space to move around.
- **Example:** "The small apartment had no elbow room."

### Every Cloud Has a Silver Lining

- **Meaning:** Every bad situation has a positive aspect.
- **Example:** "Losing my job was tough, but it gave me the chance to start my own business – every cloud has a silver lining."

### Every Dog Has Its Day

- **Meaning:** Everyone gets a chance eventually.

- **Example:** "Don't worry about the rejection; every dog has its day."

# F

## Face the Music

- **Meaning:** To confront the consequences of one's actions.
- **Example:** "He had to face the music after getting caught cheating on the exam."

## Fair Weather Friend

- **Meaning:** Someone who is only a friend during good times.
- **Example:** "I realized he was a fair weather friend when he didn't support me during my troubles."

## Feather in Your Cap

- **Meaning:** An achievement to be proud of.
- **Example:** "Winning the award was a real feather in his cap."

## Field Day

- **Meaning:** An enjoyable day or situation, often used to describe having fun at someone else's expense.
- **Example:** "The press had a field day with the politician's scandal."

## Fifth Wheel

- **Meaning:** An unnecessary or extra person.
- **Example:** "I felt like a fifth wheel at the dinner party since everyone

else was coupled up."

**Find Your Feet**

- **Meaning:** To become comfortable in a new situation.
- **Example:** "It took a few weeks to find my feet in the new job."

**Fish Out of Water**

- **Meaning:** Someone who is uncomfortable in a particular situation.
- **Example:** "He felt like a fish out of water at the formal event."

**Fit as a Fiddle**

- **Meaning:** In good health.
- **Example:** "Despite his age, he's fit as a fiddle."

**Flash in the Pan**

- **Meaning:** Something or someone that initially shows promise but fails to deliver.
- **Example:** "His first novel was a bestseller, but he turned out to be a flash in the pan."

**Fly Off the Handle**

- **Meaning:** To lose one's temper suddenly and unexpectedly.
- **Example:** "You need to learn to stay calm and not fly off the handle at small issues."

**Food for Thought**

- **Meaning:** Something to think about.
- **Example:** "The presentation provided plenty of food for thought about our future strategies."

**Fool's Gold**

- **Meaning:** Something that appears valuable but is actually worthless.
- **Example:** "The investment looked promising but turned out to be fool's gold."

**Fit as a Fiddle**

- **Meaning:** In good health.
- **Example:** "Despite his age, he's fit as a fiddle."

## G

### Get a Second Wind

- **Meaning:** To have a burst of energy after being tired.
- **Example:** "After a short break, I got a second wind and finished the marathon."

### Get Cold Feet

- **Meaning:** To feel nervous or unsure about something.
- **Example:** "She got cold feet just before her wedding."

### Get Out of Hand

- **Meaning:** To become uncontrollable.
- **Example:** "The party got out of hand when too many people showed up."

### Get Your Act Together

- **Meaning:** To organize yourself more effectively.
- **Example:** "You need to get your act together if you want to succeed."

### Give Someone the Cold Shoulder

- **Meaning:** To intentionally ignore or treat someone in an unfriendly way.

- **Example:** "After their argument, she gave him the cold shoulder for weeks."

**Go Out on a Limb**

- **Meaning:** To take a risk.
- **Example:** "I'll go out on a limb and predict that our team will win the championship."

**Go the Extra Mile**

- **Meaning:** To make an extra effort to achieve something.
- **Example:** "She always goes the extra mile to ensure her clients are satisfied."

**Grasp at Straws**

- **Meaning:** To try any solution, even if it's not likely to succeed.
- **Example:** "He was grasping at straws to find a way to fix the problem."

**Green with Envy**

- **Meaning:** Very jealous.
- **Example:** "She was green with envy when she saw her friend's new car."

**Gut Feeling**

- **Meaning:** A personal intuition or instinct.

- **Example:** "I had a gut feeling that something was wrong."

# H

## Hair of the Dog

- **Meaning:** An alcoholic drink taken to cure a hangover.
- **Example:** "He swears by a hair of the dog after a night of heavy drinking."

## Hang in There

- **Meaning:** To keep going, persevere.
- **Example:** "Hang in there – things will get better soon."

## Have a Bone to Pick

- **Meaning:** To have a complaint or grievance.
- **Example:** "I have a bone to pick with you about last night's meeting."

## Hit the Ground Running

- **Meaning:** To begin something energetically and effectively.
- **Example:** "She hit the ground running on her first day at the job."

## Hit the Nail on the Head

- **Meaning:** To be exactly right about something.
- **Example:** "You've hit the nail on the head with your analysis of the problem."

### Hit the Sack

- **Meaning:** To go to bed.
- **Example:** "I'm exhausted; I'm going to hit the sack."

### Hold Your Horses

- **Meaning:** To wait or be patient.
- **Example:** "Hold your horses! Let's think about this before we decide."

### Hot Potato

- **Meaning:** A controversial or difficult issue.
- **Example:** "The issue of immigration reform has become a political hot potato."

# I

## In the Heat of the Moment

- **Meaning:** Overwhelmed by what is happening in the moment.
- **Example:** "He said some things he didn't mean in the heat of the moment."

## In the Nick of Time

- **Meaning:** Just in time.
- **Example:** "They arrived at the airport in the nick of time to catch their flight."

## It Takes Two to Tango

- **Meaning:** Both parties involved in a situation are responsible.
- **Example:** "Don't blame him alone for the argument – it takes two to tango."

## If Looks Could Kill

- **Meaning:** Used to describe an extremely angry or hostile look someone gives.
- **Example:** "If looks could kill, I'd be dead after the glare she gave me."

## In Over Your Head

- **Meaning:** Involved in something that is too difficult to handle.

- **Example:** "He's in over his head with that complex project."

**In the Same Boat**

- **Meaning:** In the same situation.
- **Example:** "During the recession, many people found themselves in the same boat regarding job security."

**Ivory Tower**

- **Meaning:** A state of privileged seclusion or separation from the real world.
- **Example:** "Academics in their ivory towers often miss the practical applications of their research."

**It's Not Rocket Science**

- **Meaning:** It's not very complicated.
- **Example:** "Changing a flat tire isn't rocket science."

**It's Raining Cats and Dogs**

- **Meaning:** It's raining very heavily.
- **Example:** "It's raining cats and dogs outside; don't forget your umbrella."

# J

## Jack of All Trades, Master of None

- **Meaning:** A person who is competent in many skills but not outstanding in any one.
- **Example:** "He's a jack of all trades but a master of none – he can do many things but isn't an expert in any."

## Jump the Gun

- **Meaning:** To start something too soon.
- **Example:** "They jumped the gun by announcing the new product before finalizing its design."

## Jump Through Hoops

- **Meaning:** To go through a difficult or complex procedure to achieve something.
- **Example:** "You'll have to jump through hoops to get the permit."

## Jump to Conclusions

- **Meaning:** To decide something is true without having all the facts.
- **Example:** "Don't jump to conclusions; let's wait until we have all the information."

## K

### Keep an Eye On

- **Meaning:** To watch or monitor closely.
- **Example:** "Can you keep an eye on the baby while I make dinner?"

### Keep Your Fingers Crossed

- **Meaning:** To hope that things will turn out well.
- **Example:** "I have my exam results tomorrow – keep your fingers crossed for me!"

### Kick the Bucket

- **Meaning:** To die.
- **Example:** "He kicked the bucket after a long illness."

### Kill Two Birds with One Stone

- **Meaning:** To accomplish two tasks with a single action.
- **Example:** "By going to the conference, I killed two birds with one stone – I learned about new trends and networked with industry leaders."

### Know the Ropes

- **Meaning:** To be familiar with the details of a task or job.
- **Example:** "It took a while to learn the ropes, but now I feel

confident in my new role."

### Knock on Wood

- **Meaning:** Said to avoid bad luck.
- **Example:** "I've never been in a car accident, knock on wood."

## L

### Lend an Ear

- **Meaning:** To listen attentively.
- **Example:** "Whenever I need to talk, she's always there to lend an ear."

### Let the Cat Out of the Bag

- **Meaning:** To reveal a secret, often unintentionally.
- **Example:** "She let the cat out of the bag about the surprise party."

### Light at the End of the Tunnel

- **Meaning:** The end of a difficult situation is in sight.
- **Example:** "After months of hard work, I can finally see the light at the end of the tunnel."


### Let the Cat Out of the Bag

- **Meaning:** To reveal a secret, often unintentionally.
- **Example:** "She let the cat out of the bag about the surprise party."

### Lend an Ear

- **Meaning:** To listen attentively.
- **Example:** "Whenever I need to talk, she's always there to lend an ear."

### Lose Your Touch

- **Meaning:** To lose the ability or talent you once had.
- **Example:** "He used to be a great tennis player, but he seems to have lost his touch."

## M

### Make a Long Story Short

- **Meaning:** To summarize.
- **Example:** "To make a long story short, we missed our flight and had to wait for the next one."

### Miss the Boat

- **Meaning:** To miss an opportunity.
- **Example:** "I didn't invest in the stock market early on, so I missed the boat."

### Monkey Business

- **Meaning:** Dishonest or bad behavior.
- **Example:** "The supervisor warned them to stop the monkey business and get back to work."

### Move Heaven and Earth

- **Meaning:** To do everything possible to achieve something.
- **Example:** "They moved heaven and earth to make sure the event was a success."

### Mad as a Hatter

- **Meaning:** Completely insane.

- **Example:** "He's mad as a hatter if he thinks he can climb that mountain without any training."

### Make Ends Meet

- **Meaning:** To have enough money to cover expenses.
- **Example:** "With the high cost of living, it's hard to make ends meet."

### Move the Goalposts

- **Meaning:** To change the rules or targets in a way that makes it more difficult to achieve something.
- **Example:** "Every time we get close to a deal, they move the goalposts."

## N

### Neck of the Woods

- **Meaning:** A specific area or neighborhood.
- **Example:** "We haven't seen you in this neck of the woods for a long time."

### Not Playing with a Full Deck

- **Meaning:** Not mentally sound or crazy.
- **Example:** "He's not playing with a full deck if he thinks he can finish that project in one day."

### Not Up to Scratch

- **Meaning:** Not good enough.
- **Example:** "His work wasn't up to scratch, so he had to redo it."

### Nip It in the Bud

- **Meaning:** To stop something before it becomes a problem.
- **Example:** "We need to nip the rumors in the bud."

### No Dice

- **Meaning:** No chance.
- **Example:** "I asked for an extension, but it was no dice."

**No Brainer**

- **Meaning:** Something that is very obvious or easy to understand.
- **Example:** "Accepting the job offer was a no brainer."

**Nip and Tuck**

- **Meaning:** Very close in competition.
- **Example:** "The race was nip and tuck until the very end."

## O

### Off the Hook

- **Meaning:** Free from blame or responsibility.
- **Example:** "He was relieved to be off the hook after the investigation cleared him."

### On Cloud Nine

- **Meaning:** Extremely happy.
- **Example:** "She was on cloud nine after getting the job."

### On the Ball

- **Meaning:** Alert and aware of what is happening.
- **Example:** "She's really on the ball and keeps track of all the latest trends."

### On the Fence

- **Meaning:** Undecided between two options.
- **Example:** "I'm on the fence about whether to take the job or stay where I am."

### Once in a Blue Moon

- **Meaning:** Very rarely.
- **Example:** "She visits her hometown once in a blue moon."

### Open a Can of Worms

- **Meaning:** To create a complicated situation.
- **Example:** "Bringing up that old argument will just open a can of worms."

### Off One's Rocker

- **Meaning:** Crazy or insane.
- **Example:** "Anyone who jumps into freezing water must be off their rocker."

### Out of the Blue

- **Meaning:** Something unexpected.
- **Example:** "She called me out of the blue after years of no contact."

### Over the Moon

- **Meaning:** Extremely pleased or happy.
- **Example:** "He was over the moon with his new job."

## P

### Piece of Cake

- **Meaning:** Something very easy to do.
- **Example:** "Fixing the car was a piece of cake for him."

### Play It by Ear

- **Meaning:** To improvise rather than follow a plan.
- **Example:** "We don't have a strict itinerary for the trip; we'll just play it by ear."

### Pulling Someone's Leg

- **Meaning:** To joke or tease someone.
- **Example:** "Don't worry, I'm just pulling your leg."

### Put Your Foot Down

- **Meaning:** To be firm about something.
- **Example:** "You need to put your foot down and set some boundaries."

### Put the Cart Before the Horse

- **Meaning:** To do things in the wrong order.
- **Example:** "Planning the details before deciding the overall strategy is putting the cart before the horse."

### Pull Out All the Stops

- **Meaning:** To do everything possible to achieve something.
- **Example:** "We'll pull out all the stops to make the event a success."

### Put Your Money Where Your Mouth Is

- **Meaning:** To take action to support one's words.
- **Example:** "If you think it's such a good idea, why don't you put your money where your mouth is?"

## Q

### Quit Cold Turkey

- **Meaning:** To suddenly stop doing something that is usually a bad habit.
- **Example:** "He quit smoking cold turkey."

### Quid Pro Quo

- **Meaning:** A favor for a favor.
- **Example:** "It's a quid pro quo arrangement – I help him, and he helps me."

### Quick on the Draw

- **Meaning:** Very fast in acting or reacting.
- **Example:** "She's quick on the draw with her responses in meetings."

### Quit While You're Ahead

- **Meaning:** To stop doing something before it becomes worse.
- **Example:** "You should quit while you're ahead before making more mistakes."

## R

### Rain on Your Parade

- **Meaning:** To spoil someone's plans.
- **Example:** "I hate to rain on your parade, but we're not going to finish on time."

### Read Between the Lines

- **Meaning:** To understand the hidden meaning.
- **Example:** "If you read between the lines, you'll see that she's not happy with the decision."

### Ring a Bell

- **Meaning:** To sound familiar.
- **Example:** "His name rings a bell, but I can't remember where I've heard it before."

### Rock the Boat

- **Meaning:** To cause trouble or disturb a stable situation.
- **Example:** "Don't rock the boat by bringing up controversial topics at the meeting."

### Run of the Mill

- **Meaning:** Average or ordinary.

- **Example:** "It was just a run-of-the-mill performance."

### Right as Rain

- **Meaning:** In good health or condition.
- **Example:** "After a good night's sleep, I'll be right as rain."

### Run Around Like a Headless Chicken

- **Meaning:** To be very busy doing many things, but in a disorganized way.
- **Example:** "She was running around like a headless chicken trying to get everything ready for the party."

# S

## See Eye to Eye

- **Meaning:** To agree fully.
- **Example:** "They didn't see eye to eye on the issue, leading to a lengthy debate."

## Shake a Leg

- **Meaning:** To hurry up.
- **Example:** "Shake a leg, or we'll be late for the movie."

## Shoot the Breeze

- **Meaning:** To chat casually.
- **Example:** "We spent the afternoon shooting the breeze about our college days."

## Skeleton in the Closet

- **Meaning:** A hidden secret or scandal.
- **Example:** "Every family has a skeleton in the closet."

## Sleep on It

- **Meaning:** To take some time to think about something before making a decision.
- **Example:** "I need to sleep on it before deciding."

**Spill the Beans**

- **Meaning:** To reveal a secret.
- **Example:** "She spilled the beans about the surprise party."

**Steal Someone's Thunder**

- **Meaning:** To take credit for someone else's achievements or ideas.
- **Example:** "He stole her thunder by announcing the project as his own."

**Straight from the Horse's Mouth**

- **Meaning:** From a reliable source.
- **Example:** "I heard it straight from the horse's mouth – our boss is leaving the company."

**Spill the Beans**

- **Meaning:** To reveal a secret.
- **Example:** "She spilled the beans about the surprise party."

**Straight from the Horse's Mouth**

- **Meaning:** Directly from the original source.
- **Example:** "I heard it straight from the horse's mouth."

**Sweep Under the Rug**

- **Meaning:** To hide or ignore something.

- **Example:** "You can't just sweep your problems under the rug."

**Save Face**

- **Meaning:** To avoid humiliation.
- **Example:** "He tried to save face by blaming the computer for the error."

**Stick to Your Guns**

- **Meaning:** To refuse to change your beliefs or actions.
- **Example:** "She stuck to her guns and didn't compromise on her principles."

**Sitting Duck**

- **Meaning:** A vulnerable target.
- **Example:** "Without a proper defense, they were sitting ducks."

**Speak of the Devil**

- **Meaning:** When someone appears just after being mentioned.
- **Example:** "Speak of the devil, and he shall appear."

## T

### Take a Rain Check

- **Meaning:** To postpone a plan.
- **Example:** "I'll have to take a rain check on dinner; I have too much work tonight."

### Take It with a Grain of Salt

- **Meaning:** To not take something too seriously.
- **Example:** "Take his advice with a grain of salt; he's not an expert."

### The Ball Is in Your Court

- **Meaning:** It's your decision or responsibility to do something.
- **Example:** "I've done all I can; now the ball is in your court."

### The Best of Both Worlds

- **Meaning:** Benefiting from two different opportunities or situations.
- **Example:** "Living in the city and working from home gives me the best of both worlds."

### The Last Straw

- **Meaning:** The final problem in a series of problems.
- **Example:** "His rude comment was the last straw – I've had enough."

**Throw in the Towel**

- **Meaning:** To give up or admit defeat.
- **Example:** "After several failed attempts, he finally threw in the towel."

**Tie the Knot**

- **Meaning:** To get married.
- **Example:** "They're planning to tie the knot next summer."

**Turn a Blind Eye**

- **Meaning:** To ignore something that you know is wrong.
- **Example:** "The manager turned a blind eye to the employee's tardiness."

**Throw Caution to the Wind**

- **Meaning:** To take a risk.
- **Example:** "They threw caution to the wind and invested all their money in the new venture."

**Through Thick and Thin**

- **Meaning:** In good times and bad.
- **Example:** "We've been friends through thick and thin."

**Turn Over a New Leaf**

- **Meaning:** To change one's behavior for the better.
- **Example:** "He promised to turn over a new leaf and start fresh."

**Tip of the Iceberg**

- **Meaning:** A small part of a much larger problem.
- **Example:** "The issues you see are just the tip of the iceberg."

**Take the Bull by the Horns**

- **Meaning:** To deal with a difficult situation directly.
- **Example:** "He decided to take the bull by the horns and confront his boss."

**Throw in the Towel**

- **Meaning:** To give up or admit defeat.
- **Example:** "After several failed attempts, he finally threw in the towel."

**Tongue-in-Cheek**

- **Meaning:** A humorous or sarcastic statement not meant to be taken seriously.
- **Example:** "Her comments were meant to be tongue-in-cheek."

## U

### Under the Weather

- **Meaning:** Feeling ill.
- **Example:** "I'm feeling a bit under the weather today."

### Up in the Air

- **Meaning:** Uncertain or undecided.
- **Example:** "Our travel plans are still up in the air due to the pandemic."

### Use Your Loaf

- **Meaning:** To use your brain or think clearly.
- **Example:** "Come on, use your loaf and solve the problem."

### Under the Gun

- **Meaning:** Under pressure.
- **Example:** "I'm under the gun to finish this project by tomorrow."

### Up the Ante

- **Meaning:** To increase the stakes or demands.
- **Example:** "The company upped the ante by offering a better salary."

### Under Your Belt

- **Meaning:** Achieved or experienced.
- **Example:** "With two successful projects under her belt, she's ready for a new challenge."

**Upper Hand**

- **Meaning:** Advantage or control over a situation.
- **Example:** "She has the upper hand in negotiations."

## V

### Variety Is the Spice of Life

- **Meaning:** New experiences make life more interesting.
- **Example:** "Try new things and travel – variety is the spice of life."

### Vanish into Thin Air

- **Meaning:** To disappear completely.
- **Example:** "The thief vanished into thin air before the police arrived."

### Vent One's Spleen

- **Meaning:** To express anger.
- **Example:** "He vented his spleen during the heated argument."

### Vicious Circle

- **Meaning:** A problem that leads to another problem, making the original issue worse.
- **Example:** "Poverty and crime can create a vicious circle."

## W

### Walking on Air

- **Meaning:** Feeling very happy.
- **Example:** "After the promotion, he was walking on air."

### Wear Your Heart on Your Sleeve

- **Meaning:** To show your emotions openly.
- **Example:** "She wears her heart on her sleeve, and everyone knows how she feels."

### When Pigs Fly

- **Meaning:** Something that will never happen.
- **Example:** "He'll apologize when pigs fly."

### Wild Goose Chase

- **Meaning:** A futile or hopeless pursuit.
- **Example:** "Searching for her lost keys in the park was a wild goose chase."

### With a Grain of Salt

- **Meaning:** To take something lightly or with skepticism.
- **Example:** "Take his advice with a grain of salt; he tends to exaggerate."

**Wrap One's Head Around**

- **Meaning:** To understand something complex.
- **Example:** "It took me a while to wrap my head around the new system."

**Whistle in the Dark**

- **Meaning:** To pretend to be unafraid.
- **Example:** "He was just whistling in the dark when he said he wasn't scared."

**Water Under the Bridge**

- **Meaning:** Past events that are no longer important.
- **Example:** "Let's not dwell on the past; it's all water under the bridge."

## Y

### You Can’t Judge a Book by Its Cover

- **Meaning:** Don’t judge someone or something based on appearance.
- **Example:** "She looked unassuming, but you can’t judge a book by its cover."

### Your Guess Is as Good as Mine

- **Meaning:** To not know something.
- **Example:** "When it comes to understanding quantum physics, your guess is as good as mine."

### You Can't Have Your Cake and Eat It Too

- **Meaning:** You can't have two incompatible things.
- **Example:** "He wants the promotion without the extra work, but you can't have your cake and eat it too."

### Yellow-Bellied

- **Meaning:** Cowardly.
- **Example:** "He's too yellow-bellied to stand up for what's right."

### You Bet Your Bottom Dollar

- **Meaning:** To be very sure of something.

- **Example:** "You can bet your bottom dollar she'll be at the meeting."

**You're Barking Up the Wrong Tree**

- **Meaning:** To pursue a mistaken course of action.
- **Example:** "If you think I'm responsible, you're barking up the wrong tree."

Chapter 10

# Expanding Your Idiomatic Horizons

## Resources for Further Learning

Idioms are a fascinating and integral part of any language, providing a unique lens through which we can understand culture, history, and the human experience. While this book has offered a comprehensive guide to many common and useful idioms, the journey of learning and mastering idiomatic expressions doesn't end here. This chapter is dedicated to helping you continue your exploration of idioms and language, offering resources that will deepen your understanding, enhance your proficiency, and keep your learning engaging and enjoyable.

### 1. Online Idiom Databases and Dictionaries

The internet is a treasure trove of resources for language learners. Numerous websites and online dictionaries are specifically dedicated to idioms, offering extensive lists, detailed explanations, and usage examples.

### A. The Idiom Connection

The Idiom Connection is an online resource that provides a vast collection of English idioms, phrases, and expressions. The website categorizes idioms alphabetically and thematically, making it easy to find specific idioms or explore new ones. Each idiom is accompanied by its meaning and usage in a sentence, helping learners understand the context.

### B. UsingEnglish.com

UsingEnglish.com is a comprehensive resource for ESL (English as a Second Language) learners. The website includes a large database of idioms, complete with definitions and example sentences. Additionally, UsingEnglish.com offers quizzes, forums, and other learning tools to help reinforce your understanding of idiomatic expressions.

### C. The Free Dictionary by Farlex

The Free Dictionary by Farlex offers a specialized section for idioms and phrases, providing thorough definitions, origins, and usage examples. This resource is particularly useful for learners who want to delve deeper into the historical and cultural backgrounds of idioms.

## 2. Mobile Apps for Idiom Learning

In our digital age, mobile apps offer convenient and interactive ways to learn and practice idioms. Here are some recommended apps that you can use on-the-go:

### A. Idiom Land

Idiom Land is a mobile app designed to make learning idioms fun and engaging. The app features a large collection of idioms with meanings, examples, and quizzes. The interactive nature of the app makes it a great tool for reinforcing your learning through repetition and practice.

### B. English Idioms and Phrases

This app provides a comprehensive list of idioms and phrases, complete with definitions and usage examples. It also includes flashcards and quizzes to test your knowledge. The app's user-friendly interface makes it easy to navigate and find specific idioms.

### C. Quizlet

While not exclusively dedicated to idioms, Quizlet is a versatile learning app that allows users to create custom flashcards and quizzes. You can search for existing idiom sets or create your own to tailor your learning experience. The app's gamified approach makes studying idioms both fun and effective.

## 3. Books and E-Books on Idioms

Books remain one of the most reliable and comprehensive resources for language learning. Here are some recommended titles that provide in-depth coverage of idioms:

**A. "The Oxford Dictionary of Idioms"**

Published by Oxford University Press, this dictionary is a highly regarded reference book that offers clear definitions and usage examples for thousands of idioms. The entries are enriched with information about the origins and variations of idioms, making it an invaluable resource for both native speakers and learners.

**B. "NTC's Dictionary of Everyday American English Expressions" by Richard Spears**

This book focuses on idioms and expressions that are commonly used in everyday American English. It provides clear explanations and examples, helping learners understand how to use idioms naturally in conversation.

**C. "The Big Book of American Idioms: A Comprehensive Dictionary of English Idioms, Expressions, Phrases & Sayings"**

This comprehensive dictionary covers a wide range of idioms, expressions, and sayings used in American English. Each entry includes a definition, example sentences, and usage notes, making it a practical resource for learners at all levels.

## 4. Online Courses and MOOCs

For those who prefer structured learning, online courses and MOOCs (Massive Open Online Courses) offer an excellent way to study idioms in a guided environment. These courses are often interactive and include multimedia content to enhance your learning experience.

### A. Coursera

Coursera offers courses from top universities and institutions around the world. You can find courses specifically focused on idiomatic expressions, as well as broader courses on English language and literature that include sections on idioms. The platform provides video lectures, quizzes, and peer discussions to reinforce learning.

### B. edX

Similar to Coursera, edX offers a variety of courses from prestigious universities. Look for courses on English language learning, which often include modules on idioms and phrases. The interactive nature of these courses, combined with the opportunity to learn from expert instructors, makes edX a valuable resource.

### C. Udemy

Udemy offers a wide range of courses on idioms and phrases, catering to different levels of learners. The courses often include video lessons, downloadable resources, and quizzes. Udemy's flexible learning structure allows you to learn at your own pace, making it ideal for busy learners.

## 5. Podcasts and YouTube Channels

For auditory and visual learners, podcasts and YouTube channels offer engaging ways to learn idioms. These resources often provide real-life examples and contextual explanations, making it easier to understand and remember idiomatic expressions.

### A. "The English We Speak" by BBC Learning English

This podcast focuses on everyday idioms and phrases used in British English. Each episode is short and features real-life examples, making it easy to fit into your daily routine. The hosts provide clear explanations and usage tips, helping you incorporate idioms into your own speech.

### B. "All Ears English Podcast"

The All Ears English Podcast is designed for ESL learners and covers a wide range of topics, including idioms and phrases. The hosts discuss idioms in the context of American culture, providing insights into how and when to use them. The conversational style of the podcast makes it an enjoyable learning experience.

### C. YouTube Channels

YouTube is home to numerous channels dedicated to teaching English idioms. Some popular channels include:

- **English Addict with Mr. Duncan:** Mr. Duncan's channel offers lessons on various aspects of English, including idioms and expressions. His engaging teaching style and clear explanations make learning idioms enjoyable.

- **BBC Learning English:** The BBC Learning English channel features series like "The English We Speak," where hosts discuss idioms and phrases used in everyday conversation. The videos provide contextual examples and tips for using idioms correctly.
- **Rachel's English:** Rachel's English focuses on American English pronunciation and usage, including idioms. The channel's detailed lessons and practical examples help learners understand how to use idiomatic expressions naturally.

## 6. Practice and Application

Learning idioms is one thing, but using them effectively requires practice. Here are some strategies and resources to help you practice idioms in real-life contexts:

### A. Language Exchange Platforms

Language exchange platforms connect you with native speakers who can help you practice idioms in conversation. Websites like Tandem, HelloTalk, and ConversationExchange allow you to chat with language partners, providing opportunities to use idioms naturally and receive feedback.

### B. Writing Prompts and Exercises

Practice writing sentences, paragraphs, or short stories that incorporate idioms. This exercise not only reinforces your understanding of idioms but also helps you become more comfortable using them in your writing. You can find writing prompts and exercises in idiom books, online resources, or create your own.

### C. Join English Language Forums and Communities

Participate in online forums and communities dedicated to English language learning. Websites like Reddit (r/EnglishLearning) and English Language & Usage Stack Exchange offer platforms where you can ask questions, share knowledge, and practice using idioms with fellow learners and native speakers.

## 7. Engaging with Literature and Media

Immersing yourself in English literature and media is an effective way to encounter idioms in their natural context. Reading books, watching movies, and listening to music can expose you to a wide range of idiomatic expressions and help you understand their usage.

### A. Reading Books

Choose books that are rich in idiomatic language. Novels, short stories, and even comic books can provide ample examples of idioms in context. Pay attention to how authors use idioms to convey meaning and create vivid imagery.

### B. Watching Movies and TV Shows

Movies and TV shows are excellent resources for hearing idioms used in natural conversation. Pay attention to dialogue and note any idioms you encounter. Watching with subtitles can help you catch and understand idiomatic expressions.

### C. Listening to Music

Songs often contain idiomatic expressions that convey emotions and tell stories. Listen to different genres of music and try to identify idioms in the lyrics. This can be a fun and engaging way to enhance your idiomatic vocabulary.

## 8. Engaging in Creative Projects

Incorporating idioms into creative projects can make learning more enjoyable and memorable. Here are some ideas:

### A. Create an Idiom Journal

Maintain a journal where you document new idioms, their meanings, and example sentences. Illustrate the idioms with drawings or photos to make them more memorable. Reviewing your journal regularly will reinforce your learning.

### B. Write a Blog or Social Media Posts

Share your idiom discoveries and usage tips on a blog or social media platform. Writing about idioms and engaging with readers can help reinforce your understanding and provide a creative outlet for your learning.

### C. Compose Poems or Stories

Challenge yourself to write poems or short stories that incorporate idioms. This exercise not only enhances your idiomatic vocabulary but also stimulates your creativity and helps you practice using idioms in various contexts.

### 9. Cultural Immersion

Understanding the cultural context of idioms can deepen your appreciation and comprehension. Here are some ways to immerse yourself in the culture behind the language:

#### A. Travel

If possible, visit English-speaking countries and immerse yourself in the language and culture. Interacting with native speakers and experiencing the culture firsthand can provide valuable insights into idiomatic expressions.

#### B. Attend Cultural Events

Participate in cultural events, such as film festivals, theater performances, and literary readings. These events offer opportunities to hear idioms in authentic contexts and engage with the cultural nuances behind them.

#### C. Connect with Native Speakers

Building relationships with native speakers can enhance your learning experience. Engage in conversations, ask questions about idioms, and learn from their perspectives and experiences.

## Conclusion

Mastering idioms is a continuous journey that extends beyond the pages of this book. By leveraging the resources and strategies outlined in this chapter, you can continue to expand your idiomatic horizons and enrich your language skills. Whether through online databases, mobile apps, books, courses, or cultural immersion, there are countless opportunities to deepen your understanding and appreciation of idioms.

Remember, the key to mastering idioms is consistent practice and exposure. Engage with the language in various forms, seek out new idioms, and don't be afraid to use them in your conversations and writing. The more you immerse yourself in idiomatic expressions, the more natural and confident you will become in using them.

As you continue your journey, embrace the richness and diversity of idioms, and enjoy the unique insights they offer into the English language and culture. Happy learning!

Made in United States
Orlando, FL
25 November 2024